Wildlands

Adventures in some of the most extraordinary places on earth

James Frankham

Photography Michael Poliza

NEW
HOLLAND

First published in 2003 by New Holland Publishers (NZ) Ltd
Auckland • Sydney • London • Cape Town

218 Lake Road, Northcote, Auckland, New Zealand
14 Aquatic Drive, Frenchs Forest, NSW 2086, Australia
86–88 Edgware Road, London W2 2EA, United Kingdom
80 McKenzie Street, Cape Town 8001, South Africa

www.newhollandpublishers.co.nz

ISBN: 1 86966 046 3

Publishing manager: Renée Lang
Editor: Alison Dench
Text design: Alison Dench
Cover design: Nick Turzynski
Front cover photograph: Louise Oliver

A catalogue record for this book is available from
the National Library of New Zealand

10 9 8 7 6 5 4 3 2 1

Colour reproduction by Microdot, Auckland, New Zealand
Printed in China at Everbest Printing Co

Wildlands

CONTENTS

For my grandfather, who taught me to love the sea.

ACKNOWLEDGEMENTS

TRAVELOGUES LIKE THIS are rarely solitary achievements. Instead they rely upon a vast array of people contributing expertise, information and time. There were many rangers, guides, volunteers and enthusiasts who answered stupid questions, shared their extensive knowledge and ultimately added much to this book. They are still out there, monitoring, testing, observing and working like slaves to conserve the best of the planet for future generations.

Special thanks also go to Michael Poliza, who initiated the Starship Millennium Voyage and doggedly pushed it forward against incredible obstacles, somehow managing to shoot remarkable pictures of great beauty and sensitivity at the same time. This book was his idea.

The crew with whom I lived and worked became my family and friends; big love to Anne-Lise, Enrico, Michael, DJ, Caroline, Trevor, Monika, Dave, Lou, Lasse, Charles, Lisa, Diana, Brady, Birgit, Martin, Corinne and Odetta. And on *Starship* we also had a virtual crew: eight million followers logged on to the website and tracked our progress around the world, living every day with the crew and sending messages of support that buoyed us through the worst passages and longest nights.

I would also like to reiterate the appreciation of everyone involved in this project to the many sponsors, most notably Sony, Microsoft, Deutsche Telikom, Olympus, DLR, World Wildlife Fund and *Stern* magazine, without whom it would not have been possible. The commitment of these organisations to conservation of the natural world is encouraging.

Thanks to Alison who made it work and the publisher that tolerated my 'dynamic delivery'. Heartfelt gratitude to the friends who took time to read through chapters, experts who checked facts and Mary who inspired me with the right mix of sympathy and grit. Greatest thanks belong to my family who supported me with accommodation and encouragement as this writer hammered out his debut book. It may never have happened without you.

THE STARSHIP MILLENNIUM VOYAGE

ON 17 SEPTEMBER 1998 a 23-metre purpose-built vessel called *Starship* left Bell Harbour, Seattle on a 1000-day circumnavigation of the world, visiting six continents and travelling more than 75,000 nautical miles. The project aimed to document the world at the turn of the millennium.

Starship shared its discoveries from the planet's most remote corners with individuals and institutions around the globe via the internet, print, radio and television. Photos, video, sound and daily journals were transmitted from the ship by the most modern communication equipment available. In some countries, *Starship* had more computing power than the government. More than 20 kilometres of cable connected 17 computers, a digital editing suite, a terabyte of hard disk storage and a large arsenal of digital equipment. Specialist photographers, journalists and scientists supplemented the core crew and Europe's biggest news weekly, *Stern* magazine, covered the voyage with 37 feature articles.

The journey finished on 21 June 2001 in Hamburg, Germany, and resulted in two books and numerous television and radio features. Some 50,000 photographs and 600 hours of video were captured during the journey.

ACTIVE PAGES

THE PAGES of this book are alive on the internet. Journey with James as he films a documentary in the Highlands of Papua New Guinea. Find out where Michael is shooting now, how Diao the chimp is getting on in the wild and what's new on Aldabra. And what on earth is Frankham doing now? With the click of a mouse you can access video and sound captured during the voyage to animate these words and pictures. Peruse the journals of the voyage and update your contact information for the locations described in each chapter. There are new images to view, desktop backgrounds to download, articles to read, links to the best conservation resources on the net and new wildlands to learn about.

All for free.

 www.wildlands.cc

INTRODUCTION

THIS IS WHERE I grew up. Summer in the southern hemisphere, on a beach, in New Zealand. For years our family has been coming to Silver Bay, a pilgrimage by boat to a simple house alone in a small still bay on the eastern end of Waiheke Island. I learnt to row here, I learnt to sail and to swim. We made huts in the bush behind the house and fires on the beach at night. I grew up with sand in my hair and salt on my face.

It didn't take long to decide where I would write this book – in the place of my beginnings. In a tiny back room of the Silver Bay cottage I shiver in the first southerly of winter and try to put together a story about desert nomads. It's one of the many tales collected in a couple of years' adventuring on *Starship*.

The journey began with a phone call a couple of days after the turn of the millennium. Michael Poliza was looking for a crew member for the voyage. The goal was to circumnavigate the globe, in the spirit of Portuguese explorer Magellan, over three years. It provided a rare platform to explore the world, was well funded and well equipped, and driven with a fervent dedication by Poliza, the project director and photographer.

'Come down and have a look at the boat. Get here by one o'clock.'

'Where are you?'

'Akaroa Harbour. Near Christchurch.'

Quick maths. Thirty minutes to the airport, an hour and a bit on the plane, about two hours on a bus. I didn't have a plane ticket. I didn't know when the bus left or if there was space. And it was already 9 am.

'No problem.'

I arrived in time. And Michael quickly departed to meet with sponsors in Europe. I was left to deal with a multimedia wondership, to collect photos and stories, and maintain the 17 work stations that kept the project running. Michael had a reputation for throwing people in at the deep end to see how they would cope.

I did cope, and the two years that followed took me to the other side of the planet, across 40,000 nautical miles of ocean, visiting the most remote and beautiful places along the way. I had encounters with creatures I did not know existed. I met people of cultures so remarkably different to my own that I was inspired to review my motivations. I sailed the greatest seas of the world and walked in the driest deserts. I was enchanted in jungles and inspired in vast lagoons. I also saw rainforests felled to make furniture, I heard the roar of reefs being bombed for a handful of fish, and species driven to the edge of extinction by ignorant, arrogant bipeds.

And now back in Silver Bay, I recall the experiences and record them on my dilapidated laptop. It is itself evidence of a great journey. The H, D

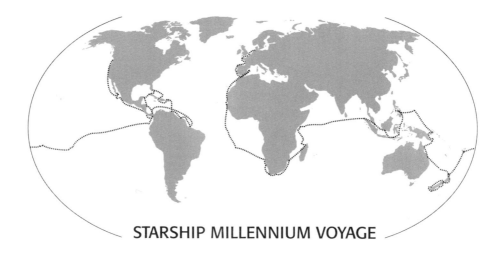

STARSHIP MILLENNIUM VOYAGE

and R keys all fell off in quick succession and the book was looking decidedly low on consonants before I got a new keyboard. I have a bag full of bits that have parted company with the machine over years of hammering, but it runs still. I'm proud of it.

Today words are hard to find. My chilly beachfront abode is at odds with images of the Namib Desert that swirl in my mind.

I opt for a cup of tea.

Morning light is reaching long inside the kitchen. The sea is glassy calm and laps gently over the sand under the deck. It's a soporific tune, complemented by the bubbling kettle. The air is clear and the light sharp; it's a typical early winter day.

The view is familiar as well. The eastern end of Ponui Island is verdant and laced with fine white beaches. Pakatoa Island rests on its haunches like a sleeping dragon and Rotoroa braces between the two, a spine of tall pines reaching skyward.

A small aberration catches my eye and I squint to focus in the distance – I could swear I saw a whale blow. But not possible.

Mist. Fin. Unmistakable…orca.

A 1.5-metre dorsal fin cuts through the satin water, scribing a long arc through a plume of breath then silently slides beneath the surface. My heart is pounding. I have never seen orcas in this channel before, let alone in front of my house. Binoculars shake in my hands and through the murky lenses I can make out another four fins.

Grabbing a digital camera I run out the door and leap into a derelict fibreglass dinghy. Long strokes through clear water. My breath heaves in sync with the oars. The whales are a reasonable distance out, perhaps half a kilometre, and I soon settle into a rhythm: stroke, draw, catch…out to sea in my clumsy craft. It's a vessel of little vanity, just a series of ad-hoc repairs. An appliance.

My grandfather used to take my brothers and me out in this dinghy to sink our glass bottles. We would punch holes through the bottoms of wine bottles with a steel rod then row 200 metres offshore and dump them, believing it was more environmentally friendly than burying them. How times have changed.

A cool breeze is ruffling the surface of the water and wavelets sparkle silver in the small vortices left by my oars. Every stroke brings me closer to the orcas. I periodically check over my shoulder for a fin or a blow. It occurs to me that my flimsy fibreglass craft will offer little protection from the curiosity of a powerful killer whale. But for the last two years on *Starship* I've been courting the most powerful creatures on the planet, and now in their company I find myself calm. I've learnt to read behaviour, to know when to move forward and when to leave well alone.

A hundred metres away a huge black fin and another plume of breath. I'm close enough to hear the powerful blow sound. It resolves my mettle, and I row slowly and quietly in the direction of the last breath. The orcas are feeding: a few minutes at the surface, and a few minutes at depth. They seem relaxed and undoubtedly sense my presence already.

I stop about 20 metres short of the group and shoot a picture. The battery light blinks. Typical. I miss the technology available on *Starship*. At any one time we had half a dozen high-resolution cameras primed with lithium batteries and long lenses.

Morning light shines wet on the fin of the largest whale. It's just a little taller than me. Dark, foreboding, breathtaking. They're relaxed, milling about in a group. Three individuals are gathered together on the surface, lolling around and breathing freely.

It is easy to identify Ben, a massive male with a propellor gash down the length of his dorsal fin. He stranded in 1987 and rescuers spent 24 hours caring for the orca before he could be returned to the sea. Ever since the ordeal, Ben has been friendly around humans in his own domain. And his behaviour has affected the entire pod, which frequently makes contact with boats.

The orcas disappear for some time, feeding at depth. I stand up in the dinghy – as my father instructed me not to – and scan the sea for any sign of them. A southerly breeze is gradually installing itself down the length of the channel and small waves patter against the hull. I'm most happy in boats. They're vehicles of adventure.

Magellan set off on the first circumnavigation with five boats and 265 men. Only one vessel returned, with 17 men on board. And Magellan was not among them. He was bludgeoned to death in the Philippines. The 17 men who survived saw the globe as none had before them. The world was suddenly smaller, more comprehensible.

More than 400 years later *Starship* completed a very similar loop. But we had modern communications and the stories were shared not only on the return to home port, but also en route via the internet. Our voyage began with a crew of six and finished with eight million, sailing with us on their home computers. And rather than a hold full of spices, *Starship* returned with 50,000 images, 600 hours of videotape and more than a thousand days of writing documenting the world at the millennium.

This book is part of that bounty. The great payload of knowledge and experience we collected along the way I sift through now. And like the tales of inspired sailors in the dimly lit halls of Magellan's *Sanlúcar*, these stories are my personal reflections of the voyage: the places, the people and the creatures that changed me forever.

The tranquillity in the dinghy is shattered. Barely 3 metres behind me comes a massive blow, like a thousand cans of soft drink being opened. I'm nearly pitched out of the boat with fright. An enormous fin rises next to my insubstantial vessel, the tip of it a few inches above my eye level. It must be Spike, a large male with a magnificent dorsal a couple of metres high.

A pulse drums in my ears and my eyes are wide. Suddenly I'm surrounded on all sides with curious orcas. Great plumes of breath blow over the dinghy, warm and stinking. Mist coats the camera lens. Another large whale surfaces vertically, spy-hopping to check me out, then slips silently back under.

I lean over the transom as a juvenile appears out of the green and rolls onto its side, so close I could touch him. He's small relative to the adults but still larger than my boat, and certainly more than capable of capsizing it with a friendly slap. We're face to face, a few centimetres of clear water rippling between us. With barely a movement he coasts past, brushing against my oar with more affection than carelessness.

The stupid camera won't focus. Out of battery, out of memory.

My heart is racing, my hands are shaking. The blows continue all around and, in truth, I'm scared. A whale passes underneath me, brushing a pectoral fin along the bottom of the dinghy. The mighty tail visible over the port gunwale, and over the starboard the defined white eye patch. The pod circles, relaxed and inquisitive. I squawk, laugh and cheer as they rise, roll and descend, hoping that somehow these primitive signs of appreciation will be recognised.

For me, conservation issues are as much aesthetic as scientific or economic. My desire for preservation is born of intrigue. Financial benefit is an unreliable measure of the need for conservation because ecological wealth is difficult to value. Not every species is of great importance to pharmaceutical research. But diversity has worth of a different kind.

We can allow the ozone layer to swell with chloro-fluorocarbons and disappear. We can watch as bandits plunder tropical hardwood forests, destroying entire ecosystems. And we can allow the precious and rare to wither and disappear. We can choose a world of stultifying sameness or preserve the diversity that we all cherish.

The locations described and illustrated in this book are among the most remarkable and ecologically significant places in the world. These places are of inestimable value. They are our crown jewels, the natural heritage of every inhabitant on the planet. And like treasure they must be protected. We are the stewards of our own inheritance.

My reflection wobbles on the surface of the water, distorting into myriad visages, like the faces of those who will follow. I hope that, staring over the side of a dinghy someday, my descendents will come face to face with a young Ben or Spike. And perhaps they too will sense the wonder and humility that I feel now, searching the depths for life.

Following pages p. 17 A chameleon eyes up lunch on Nosy Komba, Madagascar. pp. 18–19 A traditional sailing barge drifts up-river at Ilha de Fortalezza, Brazil.

lord howe island
AUSTRALIA

I LEAN ON the salty stanchion; spray is whipping the hull and darkness stealing the daylight. The twinkle of Cape Reinga's lighthouse disappears into the distance. Even though the photo doesn't turn out, the after-image of New Zealand is burnt into my memory – it will be my last vision of home for two years.

'A cyclone system has formed near New Caledonia and it's running south-east,' announces Trevor. 'Next Thursday it's forecast to increase to 35 knots with swells as high as 4 metres.' He pauses for effect. 'So we have to leave now.'

It's a four-day passage to Lord Howe Island over 1000 nautical miles

Left A red-tailed tropicbird whirls above Mount Eliza. During courtship males perform dramatic aerobatic manoeuvres to impress their mates.

of open ocean. There will be nowhere to hide should things get nasty. But, according to our best information, the moment for departure is ripe. The wheelhouse doors are locked and sealed as the surface of the water turns dark with a gathering wind. A long ground swell lifts the hull. Paraphernalia clatters in the shelves.

Though the cyclone peters out as expected, a new weather system is building out of nowhere. Sometimes the Tasman seems to have a life of its own, sucking inclement weather from the depths of the Southern Ocean. Over a 12-hour period conditions go from bad to worse. The small ship is tossed in a difficult sea and we have to alter course to minimise discomfort. The salon is a scene of destruction. Chairs are toppled and debris litters the floor. Crew members are shipwrecked in corners, finding sleep that was stolen in turbulent cabins.

But with six people crewing the passage, the effort on watch isn't too great. Two hours on, ten hours off, on rolling watches. Most are afflicted by a feeling of lethargy in the rough water, which transforms into a heaving nausea in the 'dog watch' between 2 am and 4 am. Captain Trevor takes great pleasure in reciting a popular adage at the meal table, just loud enough that the lapsed crew member marooned on the settee can hear: 'Seasickness occurs in three stages: you feel like you are going to die, you are convinced that you are dead, then you wish that you were.' A groan of affirmation issues from the miserable huddle in the corner.

And I have to admit that, despite a lifetime of yachting (my grandmother maintains I have salty blood), I'm feeling a little the worse for wear. Enrico, the crew's chef, seizes the opportunity and drops *The Perfect Storm* into the DVD player. It's a lurching saga of misadventure at sea where the heroic vessel is eventually capsized by gigantic waves – all hands lost. Germans have a terrible sense of occasion.

It's at 11 pm that I finally lose my composure. My dignity, my dinner and all romantic notions of life on the high seas are despatched simultaneously over the rail into the deep blue Tasman.

'Feeding the sharks, mate?' Trevor calls from the wheelhouse.

A wave crashes over the bow, sloshes down the side deck and swills around my pants. Insult upon injury.

*

STARSHIP STEERS herself with a GPS mapping system called Transas. Waypoints are plotted on an electronic chart and the autopilot sticks to a course calculated by the computer, which allows for current, wind and weather while the watchperson engages in other activities over the rail. In fact the greatest input required by the human component is to acknowledge any change in course with a press of a button. And a straight-line track across the Tasman doesn't even allow this moment of satisfaction.

So the rhythms of engine-room check and position logging are gleefully anticipated over the two-hour watch in the pilot seat. We monitor the engine room every hour, descending into the noisy depths to check the temperature and pressure of the beast, and feed it diesel fuel through a labyrinth of valves and transfer pumps.

All is carefully recorded on a log sheet that Trevor scrutinises for trends a few times a day. We check for leaks, for water in the fuel filters; we run the salt water to fresh water reverse-osmosis unit and swap between generators.

Occasionally a small red blip will appear under the swooping green arc of the radar and, with eyes glued to the screen in anticipation, one waits for the tiny rouge artefact to appear a second time. A surfacing whale? A small vessel? Perhaps a partially submerged shipping container? The watchperson presses eyes to the light-amplifying NiteSight, scanning the horizon for strange wave patterns, running lights or whale blows. Radio exchange or even a manual course change are electrifying possibilities. But invariably the blip disappears into the wave scatter, never to occur again despite wishing on the stars that it would. Ordinarily, however, the crew member on watch is simply dedicated to the task of bracing themselves in the pilot seat and trying desperately to avoid the numbing sensations of sickness.

The greatest cause for excitement is a whale sighting on day three. We slide past a sperm whale heaving in the swell, ventilating before a deep dive. White water crashes around the immense form. A tell-tale diagonal blow of misty air gives it away again before it disappears behind a surging breaker.

We have a camera in the wheelhouse for moments like this. I grab it, swing open the door, point the 400-millimetre lens in the general direction and unleash the chain shutter at eight frames per second. I got the photo, but it takes a little imagination to make out the whale through the waves and spray.

STARSHIP ROLLS in the long southerly swell, the stabilisers counter and we lurch back upright, broaching on the crest of the wave. Four days have become five and there is some relief when a voice finally sings over the intercom 'Land ahoy!'

Well yes...and no. Land it is, but not our destination. Ball's Pyramid reaches 551 metres straight out of the open ocean like a decaying and dislocated tooth, turreted, haunted and massive. The sheer faces approach vertical and the island dominates the horizon like the abandoned remains of a crumbling Gothic cathedral, stained with long streaks of guano, the sea thrashing at its base.

Fissures run laterally along the face of the spire, through layer upon layer of rigid black basalt and crumbling red ash, the aftermath of more than 100 separate lava flows. The great shard is all that remains of an island originally some 15 kilometres in diameter, whipped and destroyed by wind and wave. Geologists believe that the massive formation will crumble into the sea in the next 10,000 to 20,000 years. Nature seems to be struggling to maintain the miracle.

The stack is the habitat of the only breeding colony of Kermadec petrels in Australia and is also festooned with noddy terns, black-winged petrels and red-tailed tropicbirds. Masses of birds, mere pinpricks from this distance, circle the summit of their impenetrable ocean enclave. Water crashes against the base, sending plumes of spray into the air and slowly undermining the structure. No wide-angle lens can accommodate the view. It's such a dramatic sight that Kevin Costner wanted to use the location in his multimillion dollar feature *Waterworld*. However, the difficulty of satisfying UNESCO demands made the option impractical.

In 1979 Australian electronics entrepreneur and philanthropist Dick Smith claimed Ball's Pyramid for Australia. He was dropped into the sea

Ball's Pyramid is the world's tallest stack, towering 551 metres above the Tasman Sea and utterly dwarfing the *Starship*.

with fellow climbers John Worrall and Hugh Ward and swam ashore. The harrowing ascent was attempted the next day from a base camp. 'It's not the most difficult climb in the world,' he said, 'but the exposure is so fantastic, especially the sheer drops on the west face, and in some areas the rotten rock leads to adrenaline-pumping excitement. And, perhaps with the exception of Antarctica, the birdlife is like nothing I've seen on earth.' I expect it was a nice change from selling fuse wire.

CREW MEMBERS stagger from their sleep and congregate in the wheelhouse, peering through the salt-encrusted windows at a long, dark form on the horizon. It's 5.30 am, but after five days of rotating watches, time seems irrelevant.

On approach Lord Howe Island looks like a mighty fortress, more robust than the failing pyramid and protected on all sides by dark sheer cliffs that fall from craggy peaks straight into the early morning sea. It's actually crescent-shaped, and as we round the southern tip, the mountainous spine seems less ominous and more like a buttress surrounding a shining lagoon that spills out between the headlands.

Trevor raises the yellow 'Q' flag and an Australian courtesy ensign, mouth-trumpeting in ceremonial fashion. For him it is a return home and as we approach the island he gives us a quick rundown on correct

Masked boobies closely resemble their more common cousins, gannets.

Australian pronunciation; 'Put a "Y" on the end of everything. It's not a barbecue it's a barby, and it's not Monday it's Mundy, like Mundy Toosdy Wensdy Thursdy.'

The 'Aussy' captain spreads a fresh paper chart of Lord Howe Island on the table and dumps a handful of pencils, parallel rules and dividers on top. Despite the 40,000 electronic charts digitised in *Starship*'s navigation system, when things get tight, we stick to paper.

And things are getting tight. Trevor must navigate *Starship* through a minefield of coral heads that could tear a hole in the hull, then a small lagoon entrance with barely half a metre beneath the keel. To complicate matters, a 1.5-metre surf break is crashing over the reef. Twelve vessels have foundered on or near Lord Howe Island and we are determined not to be unlucky number 13.

The pencil scratches across the chart as Trevor plots the longitude and latitude for each course change, then loads that data into the navigation system.

Michael crackles over channel 73, '*Starship, Starship, Starship*. Channel seven-three. Copy'. Our project director flew ahead from New Zealand last week, and now sits in a police car on a hill overlooking the lagoon with the police constable/customs official/immigration officer John Gerits. People on Lord Howe Island tend to wear many hats.

Spray peels off the lips of crashing breakers. Trevor steers with eyes fixed on the steadily declining depth display – 0.8 metres – 0.7 metres. Because of the position of the transducer, *Starship* actually bottoms out at 0.4 metres.

With surfers riding the reef break on either side, we are glad for any extra information that will clarify the situation. Michael supplements Trevor's chart data with some local advice from the harbourmaster, who is calling over a cellphone from elsewhere on the island. 'You'll get through no worries,' he affirms. 'The entrance is a bit tight but plenty of water in the lagoon.' Then he qualifies. 'Just don't get off the transit line'. Now it's 0.6 metres. Coral creeps under the hull. The tender leads the way – 0.5 metres. I haven't seen Trevor exhale in the last five minutes.

With a cool hand Trevor brings *Starship* through the reef and into the comparative safety of the lagoon, where the depth is a more adequate 3 metres.

Gerits stamps the passports and then shakes my hand. 'Welcome to 'stralia, mate.'

IT'S BARELY DAWN. Immense granite cliffs rush out of the sea and encircle the 6-kilometre-long lagoon like arms in a great embrace. The sand is cold and a high tide washes around our feet on a quiet beach punctured by the burrows of nocturnal ghost crabs and fringed with tall pines. This island is one of 27 in the Lord Howe Group that have been protected as a World Heritage site by UNESCO since 1982. No less than 85 per cent of the main island is covered in untouched native forest that represents not only a great natural asset but also the financial prosperity of the island.

We creep into the dense palm forest, the floor littered with a tangle of fronds that crackle like gunfire underfoot. In 1870 indoor palms became fashionable in Europe, a trend that still exists today. The now world-famous kentia palm evolved in the mild climate, low light and dry atmosphere of Lord Howe Island, making it sublimely suitable for offices. Cultivating and selling nearly three million seedlings earns the island US$1.4 million annually, completely covering administrative costs – the residents pay no rates.

The season for the collection of the kentia palm seeds opens on the first Monday in March. Competition is fierce between locals, who converge on the prime spots on the island to scale the palms in seconds then slide down again, plunder in hand.

Two hundred metres from the beach an elderly man is tap-dancing on a picnic blanket. 'Doc' Watson explains that the haul this morning will yield some eight to ten bushels. At US$80 per bushel (30 kilograms), it's a fairly good morning's work for Doc, Maurie, Ken and their team of nephews, cousins and kids. 'Ya see 'em a lot in movies.' Doc dances on the stems, breaking the seeds off into a pile. 'One of the fellahs went to Canada and they had one in the foyer of the 'otel, he couldn't believe 'is eyes.'

Dean 'Ocka' Hiscox hoiks a glob of spit onto his hands, grips the trunk and shimmies up the palm with a webbing strap held between his feet, collects the stalks at the summit and slides down

Active page 29
Download a desktop background from Lord Howe Island.

again with a flourish. 'How hard can it be?' we wonder. Enrico, a gifted chef and juggler, discovers. He hugs the tree hard and scrabbles with his feet to little effect. When it comes to climbing trees he appears a bit of a sap. 'How you hold this?' he calls out, still struggling at the base of the palm. Michael somehow manages to make it to the top, using a combination of brute force and sheer determination. He recovers some seeds, the tree swaying perilously.

LORD HOWE ISLAND is located at the convergence of five ocean currents. A warm stream runs down the east coast of Australia to create the most southern coral reef in the western Pacific. Over 500 species of fish and 100 species of coral have been recorded in this area, which is a habitat for both tropical and temperate water varieties.

For seven million years Nature was left to its own devices on Lord Howe Island, and even when humans discovered it in 1788 they made little impact. For more than 40 years, only government ships sailing to Norfolk Island and American whalers bothered to visit. In December 1830 the 185-tonne whaling brig *George* ran aground just east of Mount Gower after striking a rock. The crew scrambled ashore with a chest of gold coins worth £5000, which they buried. The crew were later picked up by the brig *Mary Elizabeth* but a catastrophic landslide meant they were unable to recover the booty. A year later another ship, the barque *Caroline*, visited to search for the treasure. It was never found.

Humans didn't settle on Lord Howe until 1834. Today, cats have been banned and residents operate a dog importation policy that requires all canines to be 'rendered permanently incapable of reproducing' prior to arrival on the island. A human importation policy also exists, though fortunately for us it has less demanding criteria. The population today is only 330, and earning residential status on the island is well nigh impossible. The central business district consists of a post office, a bank, Thomson's General Store (established 1925), a tourist centre and a table of pumpkins with an honesty box for payment. To control the impact on the environment there is an upper limit of 393 tourists at one time.

Despite the legislation, the island suffers from a plight typical of island ecosystems. Species introduced by colonisers propagate wildly in highly adapted, closed environments. Ten endemic species of bird and two plants have become extinct since the arrival of humans. One of the greatest threats is the asparagus fern, which chokes the native bush and can now be found over much of the island. Volunteers are offered 'holidays' on Lord Howe to eradicate the destructive weed, paying up to US$600 for the privilege.

Ian Hutton fell in love with Lord Howe Island a couple of decades ago while on an eight-year posting with the Australian Bureau of Meteorology.

Ian Hutton carefully unravels a black-winged petrel atop Mount Eliza. Lord Howe's lagoon is visible behind him.

Since then he has written and photographed four books dealing with the flora and fauna of the island. Now he kneels on the muddy ground next to a 147-metre cliff face with his arm buried to the shoulder, as if the mountain has swallowed his hand. Hawaiian-print shirt, cricket hat. His eyes stare skyward, apparently searching the clouds for what he hopes to find underground. After half a minute he extracts his arm. Clutched in his hand is a flapping squawking juvenile black-winged petrel.

The species dwindled in number through predation by feral cats, but recently the island administration moved to eradicate the pests and the web-footed seabird is once again nesting in good numbers. Like all petrels and shearwaters, they make burrows to keep the young warm during the extended absence of the parent, who returns once a week with food.

'June '96 was the biggest flood in recorded history, June '97 was the second biggest, May of this year was the biggest windstorm and we're now having the driest month.' Meteorologists can remember stuff like that, but Ian is concerned at the trend – weather patterns are becoming steadily more extreme. And in fragile island ecosystems, unique species could die out almost overnight with a change in critical conditions.

We're high on the summit of Mount Eliza, the northern-most tip of the main island. Wind whistles through the grasses and ruffles my T-shirt, threatening to tip me over the edge with a soft shove. Blue Tasman waves slam against the foot of the cliff, encircling the island with a fine white valance. I can see two sea turtles breathing on the surface of the clear water, ready to dive.

Michael, in his role as official photographer, is tracking red-tailed tropicbirds with his 400-millimetre lens, doing his best to keep them tight in the frame as they whirl in the updraughts. They make a stunning sight, long red tails streaming, fine razor-like beaks, clean white feathers and black lines like well-trimmed eyebrows.

Anne-Lise calls me over to the cliff. She's lying on her front with her head and shoulders cantilevered over the edge. She's making squawking noises into a crevice – conducting research for tonight's website journal. I join her on the cornice, similarly prostrate, and peer into a small cave barely a metre deep. My head fills with blood and my feet feel light.

A ball of fluff has accumulated in one corner. Fluff with a beak, and what appear to be eyes: a red-tailed tropicbird in the making. New feathers protrude ugly from the down.

'She looks like a middle-aged drag queen after a rainstorm,' quips Anne-Lise.

Michael whistles and sings at the birds, trying to encourage them to perform ever more extreme manoeuvres, banging off frames and swapping between camera bodies and lenses like a photographer at London Fashion Week. The birds comply, pirouetting and diving, rising high and fast to foil their wings above the cliff, pitch forward over their primary feathers and descend to the cliff again.

Ian is shuffling around on an exposed knoll, fidgeting with tiny spiralled shells that I had been standing on all day but failed to notice. 'It's the internal buoyancy device of the squid *Spirula spirula*,' he says.

'A squid?'

'Yep. It lives at a depth of about a hundred metres most of the day.'

'So why are its internal organs spread over the top of a mountain?' (I pride myself on stating the obvious.)

'At night the squid fills these chambers with digestive gases and floats to the surface to feed. Noddy terns also feed at night, and pick them up off the surface. The food is then regurgitated for the young, including the indigestible buoyancy chambers and finally expelled as droppings up here.'

Elementary, my dear Frankham. Ian rolls the forensic evidence over in his fingertips. 'Quite incredible,' he mutters, more to himself than his troop of onlookers.

We scuttle behind the intrepid ornithologist cum botanist through a dense banyan and kentia palm forest. The ground is layered with a century's worth of palm fronds and seems a little elastic. The air is heavy with humidity and, with the exception of the footsteps of the *Starship* crew, the only sound is the twittering of Lord Howe Island white-eyes.

John Duff, a collector for the Sydney Botanic Gardens noted in 1882, 'There are probably few islands of similar size possessing so rich and

juvenile masked booby.

varied a flora as Howe Island, handsome banyan and other trees, shrubs, palms, pandanus, and dwarf ferns growing everywhere in great abundance and luxuriance.'

The same is true today, largely because the residents exist on the island sustainably, while doing their best to repair historical damage and negligence. Lord Howe Island is a microcosm of the best contemporary attitudes to the environment. And it's no surprise that this attitude has been fostered in an island environment where resources are slim and the effects of mismanagement instantly observed.

Reaching the east coast of the island, we scale the rocky cliff to Muttonbird Point, and a year-round breeding colony of the masked booby. The grassy peninsula is dotted with pairs of large white birds.

Spreading magnificent wings, one adult takes a few paces seaward, head low, wings beating hard, and rises straight up on the breeze to glide above the colony. Boobies dive out of the sky from a hundred metres up and crash into the water, spearing fish and squid with their sharp beaks.

Squeaks like that of a rusty door hinge emanate from a hole in the ground. Ian again assumes the ornithologist's pose: eyes skyward, arm deep in the belly of the hill. This time on the end of his arm is a large ball of grey fluff with a sharp protruding feature gripping his finger. 'It's the easiest way to get them,' grins Hutton. 'Just stick in your finger, let them bite it, and drag 'em out.'

Ian's expert hands carefully unpack the parcel. From each side is a folding wing and beneath the puff of thick down are two feet. Indeed it appears to be a carefully disguised bird; more exactly, a juvenile muttonbird.

In 1985 the British Antarctic Survey announced that a massive rift had formed in the stratospheric ozone layer that protects the earth from harmful ultraviolet light. The hole was caused by a catalytic reaction with chlorine, liberated from CFCs when we air-conditioned our cars, or kept our beer cold or squirted spray paint. Perhaps it was the first time that humans, or any species for that matter, had damaged the environment on a planetary scale. As a ten-year-old I was unnerved, believing the entire sky had somehow become unstable.

You would think an announcement of this gravity would have stimulated a sea change in attitudes to the environment. Just like a vulnerable, sensitive island ecosystem, the earth was showing its bones. But it didn't stick. We realised that we could buy emissions quotas from less industrialised countries cheaper than we could reduce our own pollution levels. Instead of making efforts to manage local fishing resources, we could fish in someone else's water. The island mindset, urging sustainable management, slipped silently away.

Though my Chicken Little (The sky is falling!) response has tempered with time, I still look at the grey bundle of fluff in the hands of our ornithologist with an epiphany of scale. Whatever each one of us does on a simple human level is projected six-billion-fold globally. Perhaps embracing the mentality of island societies will force a greater account-ability for environmental management and responsibility.

WILD GUIDE

Lord Howe Island remains a largely unspoilt haven for wildlife yet is accessible to adventurers of all persuasions. Catch a wave, sun on a beach, walk, wander and swim. Ian Hutton now runs regular week-long nature tours and special focus weeks such as Bird Week, Sea Week and Plant Week. You can be assured of seeing some of the most extraordinary ecosystems in the world. Some of the websites listed overleaf provide good information and Ian himself has published prolifically, swamping any Lord Howe Island enthusiast in reams of well-researched material.

GETTING THERE

It's easy. Qantas operates Dash 8 aircraft from Sydney most days and from Brisbane on weekends. Flight times are less than two hours.

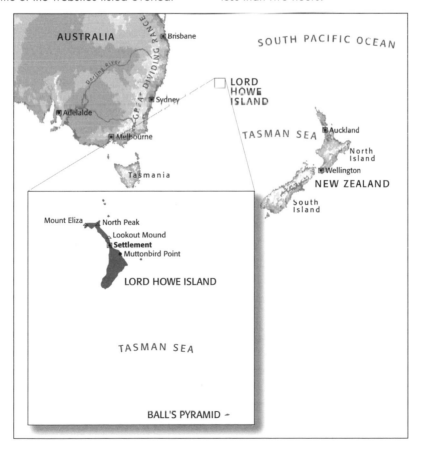

CONTACT

Ian Hutton
Lord Howe Island Nature Tours
PO Box 157
Lord Howe Island
NSW 2898
Australia
Email: lhitours@bigpond.com.au

FURTHER READING

Ian Hutton, *Field Guide to the Birds of Lord Howe Island,* self-published, 2002

Ian Hutton, *The Australian Geographic Book of Lord Howe Island*, Australian Geographic, 1998 (revised 2003)

Ian Hutton, *Ramblers Guide to Lord Howe Island*, self-published, 2002

David Doubilet, 'Lord Howe Island: Australian haven in a distant sea', *National Geographic*, vol.180 no.4, October 1991

Vincent Serventy, *Australia's World Heritage Sites*, Macmillan, 1986

WEBSITES

Ian Hutton Lord Howe Island Nature Tours
  www.lordhowe-tours.com.au
Lord Howe Island Tourism Association
  www.lordhoweisland.info
Capella Lodge
  www.lordhowe.com
Howea Divers
  www.lordhoweisland.info/services/
  howea.html
NSW Tourism Fact Sheet
  www.tourism.nsw.gov.au/media_site/
  fact_sheets/factsheetcontent.asp
  ?factsheet_id=144

Following pages *p. 37 (top)* The islands of the Lord Howe group are the shattered fragments of a volcano that erupted 7 million years ago. *p. 37 (bottom)* A masked booby stretches its 80-centimetre wingspan over the Tasman. *p. 38* Dean Hiscox scales a kentia palm with ease. *p. 39 (top)* An intriguing powder puff discovered deep underground is in fact a juvenile muttonbird. *p. 39 (bottom)* A fringing reef shelters Lord Howe Island's lagoon from a swell whipped up by storms in Antarctic latitudes. Rollers that stack up over the coral make this a great reef break for surfers.

queensland
AUSTRALIA

I LIKE AUSTRALIANS. In particular I like the variety that pervade Queensland's far north. They're coarse and buoyant in the most attractive way – always ready to throw their heads back and laugh.

Vern Jack leans back to balance his copious paunch and bellows at the crowd, 'I's the boss, I's the judge.' One hand grips a jug of beer (no glass required, mate) and the other a bewildered-looking cane toad. He started racing toads back in 1980 to raise money for the local lifeguard club.

'We're not a bank. We don't take travellers cheques, foreign currency, no plastic cards, no bids in cents.'

Left *Starship* is moored at Wheeler Cay on the fringe of Australia's Great Barrier Reef, a marine ecosystem so extensive that it is visible from the moon.

Now he's somewhat of a Magnetic Island legend, but less infamous by far than the cane toad in his left hand. It's a crude-looking amphibian: brown leathery skin, floppy legs and large poison glands protruding from its shoulders. The creature has inspired an entire subculture of enthusiasts and dopers (boiling a potful of toads liberates a disgusting but powerful hallucinogenic – apparently).

Vern straps a green ribbon around the belly of the beast and lets it hop across the courtyard. 'She knows what this job's all about.' The spectators cheer. 'Starting at five dollars only, do I hear five-a-five-a-five?'

The saga of the cane toad is a lengthy comedy of errors. Except it isn't very funny. Sugar cane was introduced to Australia as a cash crop in the late 1700s but suffered from biological attack by two species of beetle. Maybe it just wasn't meant to be there.

'Ten-a-ten-a-ten-a-ten, do I 'ear eleven? Eleven? Eleven! Eleven eleven eleven eleven dollars, twelve!'

So Queensland sugar-crofters introduced the cane toad from Hawaii in June 1935 to eat the bugs. Females lay up to 30,000 eggs in each batch and from an original landing of 101, the toads multiplied to 60,000 within six months. The breeders were delighted and released the whole lot.

'Against you, do I hear sixteen? Sixteen! Sweet sixteen!' Vern lifts the malignant *Bufo marinus* to his lips and issues a sloppy kiss. 'Sweet sixteen, never been kissed, sixteen dollars for My Green Friend.'

As it panned out, cane toads are nocturnal. And the beetles they were meant to eat are active during the day, so they never met for lunch and the programme proved useless. In fact within five years an effective insecticide became available to kill the beetles and the sugar industry lost interest in the troublesome amphibians.

Beribboned toads hop around the perspex enclosure, making desperate leaps for freedom. The Pink Pussycat is losing her skirt and Vern dutifully reties the ribbon so tight it must impede performance.

Active page 42
Race cane toads with Vern the Toadmaster! Download the video.

'Ten dollars going once, ten dollars going twice – eleven – eleven! Eleven dollars. Sold! The Yellow Rose of Texas.' No sweet sixteen kiss, the yellow-girdled beauty would have been a bargain at twice the price.

Cane toads have a long and glorious racing history. They multiplied vigorously in Queensland after the 1930s (toad begat toad begat toad) and learnt to eat all sorts of things, including frogs, then raced across Australia at a rate of 30 to 40 kilometres per year. They rank with the greatest environmental disasters on earth, establishing healthy populations over 1 million square kilometres, including Kakadu National Park, a sensitive and precious World Heritage site.

Vern rattles the enclosure and lifts it high, the toads scatter and the backpackers roar. The Pink Pussycat leads its more lethargic competitors by 2 metres. But the Yellow Rose of Texas, who seems to have paced herself better right out of the gate, bounds past with a late burst, sweeping line honours to the joy of Craig, an Irish joker who bet just 11 bucks on her form.

The Yellow Rose of Texas primes herself just minutes before her hop to victory.

Vern the Toadmaster saunters around the circle picking up the stragglers as Craig earns many a slap on the back. Meanwhile the Yellow Rose of Texas leaps to freedom under the feet of the backpackers.

Yeah I like Australians. There would be few other nationalities with the gumption and unceremonious lack of political correctness to race an environmental plague, and gamble on the outcome.

For all the humour, however, Aussies are serious about their environment and a raft of protection measures have been implemented to halt the warty march. Greatest hope is placed in a controversial virus that promises to stop tadpoles metamorphosing into toads.

Place your bets.

HE STROKES his long white beard. Leaf litter and brackish water swish around his knees. 'They rake this all up, right, and make a big mound, about a metre-twenny in width, three-quarters a metre high, lay their eggs in the top and cover it over. It acts as an inca-bater.'

'So we're standing on a crocodile nest?' I guess hesitantly.

'Yep.'

'Where's the mother croc?'

'Dunno.'

'OK…Can we go back to the boat now?'

Just in case you think I'm a girly-blouse, I browsed the United Nations Environment Programme data sheet on *Crocodylus porosus* before the outing. It described it as 'a large animal which eats humans and is aggressive when encountered near a nest'. And I just can't get comfortable loitering around up to my knees in undeniably active croc-country. It will end in tears, I can tell.

Bill Pearce has plied the waters of Hinchinbrook Island National Park, off the coast between Townsville and Cairns, all his life and knows more about the reptiles than most. He speaks with a northern twang reminiscent of cooking pots bashing together and wears giant black sunglasses with lenses like windscreens. He's everything I would expect a crocodile fanatic to be – I could have picked him from a line-up of thousands.

The sky is heavily overcast, grumbling tropical thunderclouds press down portentously. Odd sounds from foreign birds squawk through the brilliant green mangroves. The water is clear and ghostly still. A humid haze hangs in the air and gathers beneath the boughs of a soaring eucalyptus. A grand white-breasted sea eagle watches us pass.

Enrico scans the riverbank ahead with a colossal pair of binoculars. The German has rings in his nipples and a tribal tattoo that covers his entire back. And though he is probably not the sort I would normally make friends with, he is my dive buddy and we now share a special bond of trust, born at great depth, which is many times stronger than any relationship I have formed above the surface.

At NASA they send their astronauts to Antarctica with a bunch of psychiatrists to ready them for social confinement and long-distance travel. We had no such

Bill Pearce doesn't seem concerned that he's standing next to a crocodile nest.

preparation for *Starship*. Instead crew members left their families and friends, risking well-paid careers only to be dropped into floating incarceration with seven complete strangers of different cultural and professional backgrounds. On a 23-metre vessel there's nowhere to hide and getting away from your shipmates would mean drowning. But no complaints – I have come to love these strangers, even depend on them for my life.

We all fill a number of different roles to transmit the day's experiences to those following on the internet. I am the video editor, web designer and videographer, sometimes picking up stills cameras to shoot. On board we also have a diesel mechanic and captain, mate, chef, deckhand, journal writer – and Michael, the photographer and project director.

The engines putter, gently pushing the tender upriver. Michael grips the wheel in one hand and the throttles in the other. He is a protagonist, somehow concentrating the right measure of enthusiasm and famous German intensity to meet the project objectives. 'Snooze and you lose' is his favourite maxim. It's inspiring and exasperating. For hour upon hour we totter up and down the muddy channels between the sprawling mangroves, searching hopelessly for crocodiles. We're wet, cold, tired and hungry. But it's a familiar state on *Starship*, largely because Michael won't rest until he's got the shot.

Bill has elevated his windscreens to balance on top of his head and presses a pair of binoculars to his eyes. 'It's just a log,' he mutters. Actually it's the third log we have successfully identified this morning.

'Because the sun hasn't come out all that much, right, the crocs'll be a blacky-brown dark colour, right.'

'Right.'

'Once they've been laying out there a while, right, and the sun dries 'em, they'll actually turn a light grey, so they're really easy to see.'

'Like a light-grey log.'

'Right.'

Australia's estuarine crocodile has been looking like a light-grey log for well on 65 million years. The basic body plan has not really changed, as if Nature created the perfect eating machine right off the bat.

Well, I suppose. I've never seen one before and can barely contain my enthusiasm. The 400-millimetre lens is locked on the Canon and I'm scanning the banks, puffing like a stalker. It's amazing how many crocodiles one's imagination can create from mud, logs and trees. Even strange waves are contenders for optimistic transmutation.

> Active page 46
> Go croc hunting with Bill Pearce. Download the video.

The tide is dropping, revealing a tangle of mangrove roots like a haunted wooden labyrinth. Bill shows us some tiny ants on a looking-glass mangrove. 'The Bandyin Aboriginals eat those.'

'Get out of here, mate.'

'It tastes like lime.' He whips a handful off the tree. 'Try one.'

Not waiting for my response he gets stuck in, biting the green abdomen off and discarding the rest. So I give it a crack and, yes, it tastes like lime. But it's barely a speck – nothing that could sustain a people for 40,000 years. I'm sure I exerted more energy reaching out to pick it up than the total calorific value of the insect.

Bill reaches up and plucks a large heavy fruit from the aptly named cannonball mangrove. From his trousers he draws a giant knife and the ball is promptly dissected, revealing a network of peachy coloured seeds. I imagine if I dissected my own head – obviously an improbable analogy – I would see much the same pattern.

These mangrove seeds are also called monkey-puzzle nuts, as the carefully weighted seeds will only fit together one way. One by one the whole crew have a crack at trying to reassemble it. It makes monkeys out of all of us.

Red fiddler crabs shuffle backward and forward through the mangrove tangle, brandishing their out-sized right pincers.

Chef Enrico spots a crocodile. Which after a very short chase, appears to be mud. Thanks, Enrico – stick to your cooking.

The largest recorded 'salty' was over 7 metres long, and there are something like 15,000 of them in Australia, making this the best place on earth to look for a crocodile, or be eaten by one. The species has thrived under protection in Australia since the early 1970s, whereas elsewhere populations have been seriously depleted.

According to Bill we should be looking for a beast in the region of 4 metres long and just under half a tonne. They'll eat pretty much anything that crosses their path, whenever it crosses their path: fish, turtles, horses, cattle, humans. Given half a chance they'll even chomp up juvenile crocs. They're undiscerning and swift, purely opportunistic feeders. Like a few humans I know.

It's Anne-Lise that eventually spots the real thing, carefully pointing out a serrated log she's been studying for some time. On the muddy bank 250 metres away is a lengthy light-grey log of not-uncrocodilian form. Bill is quick to confirm, 'It's a salty, a big 'un.'

I am transported 65 million years back in that second, watching a giant reptile bask on the bank of the ancient estuary amidst the mangroves. The features are rugged, primal, as if thrown together by a mechanic hell-bent on making the thing last an eternity. The teeth are too large for the mouth and hang ominously out the sides in a permanent grin of satisfaction. The lumpy snout extends in a solid V to accommodate the massive head, and the rest of the animal appears to be neck. The skin is coarse and patterned with cartilaginous corrugations from the tip of the snout down the back to the tail, which resembles a dangerously

An estuarine crocodile, spooked by the boat, dashes for the safety of murky water. A crocodile's teeth are not designed to chew but to hold prey. The croc will drag it (or him/her) underwater and swallow whole or thrash into manageable bits.

serrated steak knife. The legs look like an afterthought, too small by far to be effective and jammed on the side as mystery attachments.

It's a menacing sight and, though it spots us from some distance, it seems unconcerned until we get to 20 metres away. With more grace than I would ever have thought to attribute to a 4-metre reptile, it slithers down the bank in a shower of dirt, slipping into the water with barely a ripple, grinning all the way.

Spellbound. Transfixed. My mouth is open, particles of ants hang from my teeth. The flavour of lime will always remind me of crocodiles.

FLINDERS CAY looks like little more than a remote sand bank – at best a nice place for a picnic. We pack some beverages and escape the dull rumble of *Starship*'s generator for the evening.

Flinders Reef is not a part of the Great Barrier Reef proper, it's an atoll anchored off the continental shelf in water 1000 metres deep. Though it covers 1000 square kilometres, the only exposed section is a tiny lump of sand 100 metres across occupied by boobies, terns, frigatebirds and hermit crabs. A shiny weather station squats in the middle of the cay like an abandoned lunar module.

And after sitting here for some time we realise that it doesn't even particularly lend itself to a picnic. The sand smells funny, the ground is lumpy, birds are stealing the baguette with regularity and the hermit crabs silently shuffle through the hummus. As the sun starts its dive towards the sea, the boobies go apoplectic, competing for space on the lunar module. The losers are driven away and, seeking somewhere to roost, attempt drastic landings on our heads.

Rich doesn't have a great deal of hair and is a sought-after landing site. One particularly coordinated masked booby executes a stunning low-speed descent to sit quite happily on his head, much to the amusement of the crew. Rich sips on his drink monitored from above by the gatecrasher.

The sky over the Coral Sea turns a brilliant shade of orange and I get the distinct impression of the lights dimming in preparation for a cinematic epic – the hush of excitement, the rustle of popcorn and the grand title sequence before the plot unfolds. The stage is set, and beneath the lumpy white terrain a cast of thousands is bracing for the curtain.

Moments after dark the sand begins to shift. 'Over here,' calls DJ in the darkness. Five torchlights converge from around the cay on DJ's wildly thrashing lamp. Erupting from a sandy crater are thousands of baby green turtles.

I am half expecting them to come out in single file. I expect them to take more time, to be more, well, turtle-like. But they have more in common with over-wound clockwork toys. The front flippers beat mechanically in wild swirling circles, flapping out of the sand. In a tremendous prison-break they pour over each other, exuberantly clambering up the wall of one crater and tumbling down the face of the next. Running for their lives.

What is more impressive is that they all know exactly where they are going. Bury me for eight weeks in a sand-pit and (if I ever managed to climb out) I wouldn't have the foggiest idea which way to run. Without exception the turtles make a beeline for the ocean. Boobies and terns whirl overhead, plucking the not-so-quick and the unlucky straight off the beach. The water thrashes with activity. Juvenile sharks and trevally line up along the shore awaiting the feast delivered nightly to the doorstep. The soft shell of the hatchlings does little to protect them.

Statistically less than one hatchling in 80 will survive to adulthood. And it seems their odds of survival are getting worse. Five of Australia's six species of turtles are on the endangered list and with the continuing destruction of the turtles' habitat, entanglement in nets and lack of protection in the Indo-Pacific, their long-term survival is doubtful.

The sad truth is that the 2000-kilometre-long Great Barrier Reef is being treated with some disrespect. Less than 5 per cent of the park is fully protected. So you can fish in it, you can redevelop it for hotels, seismic survey it for oil and even blow it up for military target practice. Trawling for prawns destroys up to ten times more creatures than are actually harvested, and the by-catch includes turtles and dugongs. Even more significantly, huge areas of the rich seafloor are destroyed. There are also concerns that growth in shipping traffic in the Great Barrier Reef lagoon will increase the likelihood of a major oil spill, the effects of which would be catastrophic. For all the birds and patrolling sharks, it may well be the picnicking humans that are the greatest threat to the tiny turtles before us.

The lunar module glints under our torchlights; it knows something we don't – the barometers inside the weather station have taken a sudden dip. Cyclone Tessi is developing 880 kilometres ENE of us and, as if taking aim, is moving at a steady pace WNW. Currently she is a Category 1 cyclone with winds expected up to 125 kilometres per hour. Time to run and hide.

EIGHTY-NINE YEARS ago today the 122 crew and passengers of the steamboat *Yongala* didn't have the benefit of satellite photographs or electronic synoptic forecasts to warn them of approaching danger. They didn't even have a radio. The vessel was laden with cargo and a horse called Moonshine on an overnight passage from Mackay to Townsville. She never arrived and wasn't found until 1953, some 30 metres deep in a shipping lane 45 nautical miles from her destination, where she rests right below us now.

Starship rumbles with filling dive tanks. Hoses, regs and wetsuits are strewn across the aft deck. It is the first solo dive for Enrico and me, and we fumble through the pre-dive checks nervously. Air, BCD, weight belt. Trevor, the captain and today our dive instructor, watches with a smirk. 'Where are your fins?'

'Fins, right, ah…here.'

He seems to adhere to the In At The Deep End With Mild Supervision theory of education. The wreck starts at a depth of 25 metres in open ocean with a swift current necessitating the use of descent lines. 'How long have you got at 27 metres?'

'Twenty-two minutes, no de-co,' replies Enrico.

'Right, now you guys are running this dive, and I'll just be watching.' And to instil the fear of God into us: 'Be careful, experienced divers have died on this site before.'

We find good reason for a quick recheck, and shuffle onto the aft platform. Butterflies are performing great feats of aerobatics in my stomach but I find focus in the long horizon, take a deep breath through the regulator and step off into the Coral Sea.

My mask fills with water. The large orange buoy marking the descent line bounces against my head as I compose myself. I empty my mask like the learner I hoped I wasn't and give Enrico an OK. Air hisses out of our BCDs like a couple of scared cats and we sink below the surface, the line leading into the blue. Staring into the massive abyss is a feeling akin to vertigo, except the prospect of falling is infinitely more attractive. So attractive in fact that sometimes you have to control your mind to avoid spinning down endlessly into the depths.

I follow Enrico down the line, pinching my nose to equalise the pressure in my ears. Bubbles plume from his reg and sparkle on my mask. Every so often I can see my own reflection in the face of a bubble wobbling up towards me. The massive form of the *Yongala* looms ahead of us. I feel like I'm creeping into a graveyard late at night.

The descent line is tied off at the bow of the vessel, which stretches out capsized and rusted for 110 metres. The hull is encrusted with sponges and soft corals of a thousand colours. Purple coral and blue coral, tiny yellow damselfish and orange sponges. A school of jacks loiter in a bundle surrounded by a dozen varieties of baitfish. Apart from the general form of a ship, the *Yongala* has been lost forever, covered over with a living wreath. All the mourners in the world could not have constructed as beautiful a commemoration. It's a fitting catacomb.

A hawksbill turtle, nicknamed Oscar, cruises the hull, nibbling at corals of fancy. Chevron barracuda, striped like convicts, amble in a posse looking for trouble. The wreck functions as a cleaning station, and as we watch on, Tierra batfish pull in for maintenance. They are large white dish-shaped fish with a couple of faded brown stripes crossing their face like they've been run over by a car. Before our eyes the fish change to a dark brown, revealing the lighter-shaded parasites for the cleaner fish to prise off; then with no apparent effort whatsoever they transform to a brilliant white and are relieved of dark parasites.

"oscar"

Enrico and I follow the current down the length of the ship and begin to feel like we are being shadowed. A dark form the size of a small car dips in and out of visibility. A thousand baitfish orbit the giant Queensland grouper – we weren't surprised to find out later it has been nicknamed VW. Rich hovers behind the video housing recording the spectacle on tape, the wide-angle bulb like a giant glass eye.

It's a sensational dive and as we near the giant propeller at the stern we're tempted to do the loop again. On further consideration, knowing that if we stay at this depth any longer our blood will irreversibly hyper-saturate with nitrogen and turn to froth as we approach the surface, we decide to stick to the tables and slowly ascend.

On a deep dive it's necessary to stop 5 metres short of the surface for about three minutes. It's a safety stop to reduce the chance of decompression sickness but it also allows some pause for thought. Enrico and I hover in the blue, meditating on all we have seen 20 metres below.

It is ironic that one of the greatest miracles of the Great Barrier Reef seems to have been born out of one of the greatest disasters. The *Yongala*

Xenia soft coral – poisonous to many fish

is a silent monument to Nature's durability, to its adaptability in a changing environment. More than that, it is a superb example of ecosystem resilience. That is, the capacity of a healthy environment to return to its previous state after disturbance or stress. It relies almost entirely upon the abundance and variety of species to spread the stress load.

A healthy ecosystem with high biodiversity – like the Great Barrier Reef – is surprisingly robust. Multiple species form complex and interdependent relationships within a reef system, making the value of the whole greater than the sum of the parts. A sick or habitat-depleted ecosystem by contrast has a dramatically reduced ability to recover from disturbance. In fact species are so dependent on each other that the demise of one may well bring down the entire network. But to see the resilience of the Great Barrier Reef is heartening. Large tracts of wilderness are still intact – the situation is bad but far from hopeless.

Goby camouflaged against coral sand

Enrico and I emerge to a better world than we left. A more durable planet. A planet where, if we can preserve the ecological integrity of key areas, they can look after themselves.

WILD GUIDE

MAGNETIC ISLAND

Vern the Toadmaster works from a backpackers and bar called Arkies on Magnetic (+61-7-4778 5177) most nights. Go to bet or go to watch. Ferries run from Townsville in North Queensland. Passengers only can catch Sunferries Magnetic Island ferry, which runs up to 15 times a day. The Magnetic Island Car and Passenger ferry carries

vehicles. On the island the best way to get around is in a rented Moke, a beach buggy with a temperamental clutch.

HINCHINBROOK ISLAND NATIONAL PARK

At last count Hinchinbrook was Australia's largest island national park. The drier east side, hidden behind the mountains, has long beaches separated

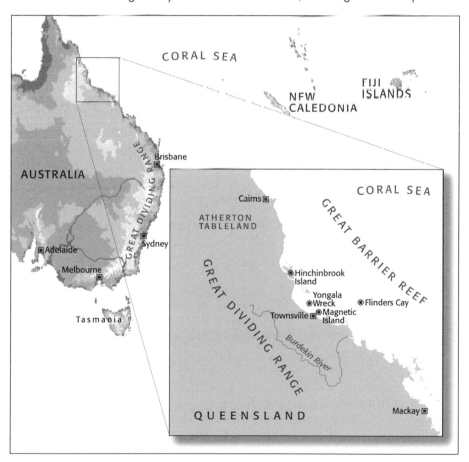

by headlands. This was Giramay Aboriginal land, but since the nineteenth-century 'dispersals' the island has not been occupied – apart from an insular resort – and Hinchinbrook remains much as it was 200 years ago. Just head north from Townsville on highway 1 to Lucinda, a little spot with a store and a few homes scattered around a sugar-loading jetty. The ferry to Hinchinbrook goes from here. Bill Pearce lives at 48 Patterson Parade in Lucinda – knock on his door if you want a tour. The 30-kilometre East Coast Trail is manageable in two to three days' walking. Catch the ferry from Lucinda to George Point. But be prepared, it rains frequently year-round.

GREAT BARRIER REEF

Mike Ball Dive Charters (+64-7-4031 5484) operates from Townsville and has a seven-day Coral Sea expedition visiting both Flinders Reef and the *Yongala* wreck. Divers will stack away around 25 dives in that time in some of the most unspoilt locations on the famous GBR. All the dive charter operations come at a price because the best sites are more than 100 nautical miles offshore, closer to the edge of the Barrier Reef.

FURTHER READING

Roger Steene, *Coral Seas*, Firefly Books, 1998

WEBSITES

Tourism Queensland
    www.tq.com.au
Magnetic Island Information
    www.magneticislandinformation.com
Walkabout Australian Travel Guide
    www.walkabout.com.au
Hinchinbrook Shire Council
    www.hinchinbrooknq.com.au
Mike Ball Dive Charters
    www.mikeball.com
WWF Great Barrier Reef Project
    www.gbr.wwf.org.au

Following pages *p. 57 (top)* Chevron barracuda orbit in search of prey. (Photo: Brandon Cole) *p. 57 (bottom)* A hatchling green turtle emerges from the nest in the early morning. In daylight latecomers will almost certainly be picked off by birds before even reaching the sharks. *pp. 58–9* The Flinders Cay weather station waits among brown boobies for Cyclone Tessi.

solomon sea
PAPUA NEW GUINEA

STEAM RISES from the jungle and our feet squish through the muddy puddles that remain after a night of torrential rain. Thunderclouds hang over Milne Bay and deep rumbles warn of more inclement weather.

Excited children run ahead, leading the way with squeals of laughter and calls of 'dim-dim'. It's a glamorous term meaning 'long pig', first given to the Spanish colonials that landed here in 1511. Today it is a veiled term of endearment that arouses curiosity among the younger children, some of whom have never seen white people. In a strange reversal of the Pied Piper fairytale we follow the singing children into a large clearing. Here small huts are constructed of local rosewood with

Left The Killia High School Philharmonia gives a rousing rendition of 'Jabba-Dae' in a classroom during a thunderstorm.

A schoolmate dots lime onto the face paint of a young warrior for Traditional Day. Designs vary remarkably from village to village.

raised sleeping platforms that remain cool and dry. Steep gabled roofs of thatched grass shed the rain.

On the small balconies children are daubing paint on each other. Once a week, on 'Traditional Day', students dress in costume to learn dances and songs as well as regular classes of English, mathematics and social studies. Fantastic patterns are being created in three colours on the faces of excited kids: black from burnt coconut husk, white from powdered coral and red from crushed seed pulp. A black base denotes *giyo* or warrior status and a red base is for *kaiwabu* or non-warrior. White dots are added in complex patterns representing tribal totems such as an eagle or crocodile.

Rain begins to clatter on the palm fronds again and we follow the sound of drums to a line of large huts. Each is a classroom. Assembled outside the largest is a mob of young boys wearing banana-leaf loincloths and armbands stuffed with green leaves. Brows furrowed in concentration, they rap out a complicated rhythm on drums made from large sections of bamboo and stretched plastic skins. Forty boys drum to the same beat and the heavens open, rain joining the percussion, hammering on the corrugated-iron roof. Groups of girls wearing grass skirts shelter beneath brilliant-green banana leaves and dance.

Competing with thunder, lightning, bucketing rain and jungle drums the teacher organises the (still dancing and drumming) students into groups. The drumming finally eases. Rain punishes the roof. A strong melodic voice from the back calls the first line of a favourite song. The class answers in unison then breaks into compelling harmony, singing for all they're worth. A spine-chilling wave of energy explodes in the tin-roofed hut and rises above the thunder and rain, dragging the inhabitants with it in a clapping, singing, drumming cacophony.

This moment will never leave me. It demonstrates in the most profound way the eagerness of Papua New Guinean youth to acknowledge their heritage and reinforce its place in their culture. The enthusiasm of the children is moving. I feel a connection to these people, and perhaps even a little sadness that my own culture has suffered so badly from the homogenising effects of globalisation.

Anthropologists believe that migrants from Asia settled this part of the Malay Archipelago some 50,000 years ago. However the only common languages are English and Tok Pisin, which is derived from English and German and developed on plantations. Generally communication is very difficult as there are more than 700 distinct languages; some villagers cannot understand their neighbours. And it is exactly this communication discord that has protected villages in the province of Milne Bay from cultural homogeneity so eager subscribed to in the capital.

Michael snaps the very first school photograph ever taken of Killia High School and the children set to painting our faces with quite unnerving vigour. Dave gets a two-tone design, Lou displays a spider-like number that appears to be taking over her face and I end up with a halo around my right eye and a volume of foliage stuffed into a headband. While traditional dress, or *bilas*, looks quite impressive on indigenous Papuans, we do feel somewhat ridiculous. Michael seizes the opportunity to immortalise us at our most ludicrous and rolls off a barrage of photos. One can only hope they never get published.

Tonight the website hums with activity. Followers from around the world eagerly download mp3 tracks of the Killia schoolchildren singing and the inbox is flooded with enthusiastic responses. There's something about the immediacy of music that communicates the spirit of a people most effectively.

The experience also helps to refocus the *Starship* crew to its task. This is what the project is all about: sharing stories of the earth's farthest corners and promoting awareness of other cultures and ecosystems. The website is by far the most important product of the voyage, with thousands living our journey vicariously. Many begin their days by switching on the computer, making a cup of coffee and then reading the latest from *Starship*. Some want to know about daily life for the crew – where we get meat, or how we wash our hair. Children send emails with questions about marine biology for their school projects, and teachers read the daily entries out to their classes. Travellers log in to use our notes as a travel guide for the daring, and retired servicemen send long-winded diatribes recounting their experiences in these waters during the war.

For some it seems to be a form of escape from difficult lives, for others a voyage to parts of the world they had never dreamed of seeing. When one of our followers goes into hospital with kidney failure and heart problems, his family prints the journals to bring to him. One woman in Washington state reads them out weekly to her 'lunch bunch', a group of eight old birds who reflect on the century and send panicky emails when we are going through bad weather.

Some of our most avid enthusiasts refer to us almost as part of their family. And when one of our crew members loses her mother there is a flood of condolences that keeps our server downloading email for hours. We have created an international community, a cult following of arm-chair travellers who live through every rough passage and every great triumph. And when the project is at its most demanding, when I feel far from family, friends and the ease of familiar society, their electric encouragement buoys my spirit.

*

DICK DOYLE lounges on his balcony. His waterfront property on Garove Island looks over the Bismarck Sea. Dickie was born in Rabaul, a town on the neighbouring island of New Britain. He lived there for some time before settling down in his own piece of paradise, where he harvests copra and cocoa.

Dick is the only white man in an island group of some 4000 indigenous Papua New Guineans. He speaks Tok Pisin fluently and has become a tribal elder of sorts. He carries with him an inexplicable patience, yet his eyes dart from side to side in excitement as he tells his stories, revelling in the opportunity to share something of what he has found.

He's a pleasant-looking guy with a white goatee and complexion that hints at a red-haired past. His daughter was Miss Papua New Guinea a few years back, he confides, clearly trying to conceal feelings of complete responsibility. Books, dog-eared and well-thumbed, are scattered across a low table with old newspapers and maps of strange coastlines.

Dick Doyle reclines in paradise. A hundred metres from his doorstep is one of the finest reefs in PNG, known to divers simply as Dickie's Place.

All manner of oddities hang from the walls, including a tiny bat that has taken up residence for the last week and a half. Wooden chairs with sagging cushions lounge decrepit on the deck. Paint peels from the weatherboards encircling the large veranda from which he surveys his kingdom. A long grassy slope hemmed with tropical plants inclines towards the water past a looming fig. A Toyota Hilux rusts quietly in the garden.

Despite the remote location we are mixing in illustrious circles: months earlier he had been visited by the software tycoon Paul Allen aboard his luxury mega-yacht. Allen and his guest Peter Gabriel, of song-writing fame, shared a beer with Dickie on his balcony. Asked if there was something he really missed being this far from 'civilisation', Dick replied, 'A ticket to the Superbowl would be good.' Weeks later he was sitting on the bleachers with popcorn-consuming Americans who had never heard of Papua New Guinea.

Doyle pats the seat of a Harley Davidson 883 Sportster propped up under the house. He explains that the island has no roads, so he gives her the gun along the length of the grass airstrip. 'It's just long enough to get her up to 93 miles an hour before you have to stand on the brakes.' He grins enormously with his hand on the chrome.

'There'll be a bit of a do tomorrow.' Dick says, rubbing his goatee, and I sense that great antipodean facility for understatement surfacing under his Australian smile. We arrange to meet the following morning.

AIR NIUGINI advertises PNG as 'The Land of the Unexpected', an epithet that has proven to be true over and over again for the *Starship* crew. And today is no different.

I stare into a waterproof bag at a loss to know what to pack. So far it contains VHF portable radios for ship-to-shore communication, half a dozen spare video batteries, as many DVCAM tapes, and a vast array of cameras, lens adaptors and cleaning cloths. A MiniDisc recorder and dynamic microphone complete the arsenal. Stuffed on top is the usual array of 30+ sunscreen, hat, jacket, gaffer-tape, bottled water and a packet of diabolical local biscuits called Liklik Wopa. They taste

Enrico, Dave and I chat to Goba children on the aft platform of *Starship*. Ballpoint pens, *National Geographic* magazines, old T-shirts and glass jars win friends but ice cubes are the showstopper – the squeals can be heard for miles.

filthy but have a marvellous capacity for filling an empty stomach.

It's clear and still. Dick is waiting on the shoreline beneath the palms. Small waves hiss over a pebbled bank. 'It's gonna be hot,' he mumbles in a prophetic tone, hurdling into the tender. Michael eases the throttle forward and the engines whine, churning the clear water to foam. The GPS registers 30 knots and Dick grins, wind-tears streaming horizontally from his eyes.

In the distance two small boats roll. Drums echo across the calm water. Men with painted faces sing loudly, chanting and dancing from the pair of 5-metre vessels. One man with a strong voice and large green hat bails furiously to keep the older of the two craft afloat. Dick explains that the more buoyant vessel is a new water-ambulance – the only connection between the remote Witu group and medical facilities on New Britain three hours south. Its arrival is the reason for today's *sing-sing*, or traditional celebration.

People living all over the Witus are converging on the Paruru Island hospital for parades and dancing. Two long dugout canoes, each with eight paddlers, join the procession, escorting the new water-ambulance towards shore. And following behind, swaying under the load of passengers clinging to every surface, is a small yellow ferry. The name 'Klaus' is written in strict letters across the stern, an obvious nod to the German colonial history of this, the Bismarck Sea. The overloaded craft is festooned with enormous bunches of flowers, and plumes of acrid smoke puff from a rusty exhaust stack that sticks straight up through the deck. The passengers call out with glee, some even risking their precarious grip for a quick wave.

Lining the beach are an odd assortment of local boats and an army of fizzing children, swarming like bees from one end to the other. Admirers immediately swamp the pageant of vessels. As I lumber ashore under a burden of equipment, little devils swing from my arms and compete for the right to carry the tripod.

Dick is absorbed into the milieu and disappears, leaving us with several thousand jumping Papuans and $30,000 worth of electronics. But I have never felt threatened in the islands of PNG. The soft faces offer enormous grins of welcome and a couple of young guys in colourful wooden hats and grass skirts help tote the equipment around. In fact by the end of the afternoon they have become quite adept at setting up a tripod and changing the lens on a Canon EOS-1N camera. The only English they understand is 'yes', 'wide-angle' and '400-millimetre, please'.

In the thick jungle behind the hospital a dance troupe waits to perform. One joker with a bushy beard wears white face paint and around his green-painted ankles are decorative lumps of orange grass. Strips of carefully threaded palm frond hang from his neck, and in his hands is a bright red electric guitar. On the other end of the guitar cable his counterpart sports a giant amplifier around his neck. The rest of the group joins into their simple riff, dancing and chanting. The war-painted children are particularly exuberant, their bodies washed with white clay and faces darkened with charcoal. They wail with gusto.

A queue of sorts has formed from the jungle to the ceremonial ground next to the hospital. Four groups of dancers are whipping themselves into a frenzy of pounding and wailing while the village elders go through some formalities. A hush is called while the austere flag-raising ceremony takes place. A group of school children in immaculate white shirts sings the national anthem as a teacher raises a tattered red, black and gold ensign. All is quiet save the angelic voices of the pupils. A thousand eyes follow the scraggy material as it gradually ascends the flagpole.

I notice a general countenance of reverence combined with puzzlement. It's as if the independent democratic state of Papua New Guinea is respected but not completely understood. It's a good thing, they've been told, and probably had many a *sing-sing* in celebration of the fact. Yet the relevance to the people of the Witu Group is just a little questionable.

A large man with a striped shirt and a bad tie mounts the makeshift speaking platform and begins a speech in Tok Pisin. As the local member of parliament, he makes sure people know who paid for the boat. A string of dignitaries follows, each claiming some level of responsibility for the gift. Well-rehearsed clapping follows each lengthy monologue. Youngsters squirm under the bright sun. My tripod boy is missing in action.

The lead guitarist of WNB Culture Group

I'm feeling a bit frazzled. The hospital doorway is shady and I prop myself up for a breather. An equally frazzled-looking charge nurse smiles at me. She is assisted by eight local nurse-aides and between them they see upwards of 500 people a month. Ten to 15

Active page 70
Listen to the WNB
Cultural Group.
Download the mp3.

babies are born in that time and medical supplies arrive once every two months. And now she has to cope with a thousand people with heat-stroke and a *dim-dim* asking stupid questions.

The drumming resumes, indicating an end to the campaigning and a start to the festivities. First up, 20 guys in wooden hats. 'WNB Culture Group' is emblazoned across the front of the elaborately carved headgear, which resembles a Bird of Paradise with two big crocodiles sticking out where a brim should be. Each is painted in vivid red, blue and yellow, and must weigh several kilograms. They wear a uniform of yellow grass skirts, green paint on their chests and thick red dirt on their faces. They clearly couldn't agree on coordinated footwear and have donned every variety of dilapidated sandshoe in various states of repair. The more authentic abandon footwear altogether. The WNB boys are going for an orchestral approach: acoustic guitars, ukuleles, drums and an electric guitar.

Group after group of extraordinary costumes and remarkable dancers parade past my camera. Each is a vibrant testimony to the diversity of PNG islanders, separated not only by water but also by culture. Every tiny island has its own ceremonial dress and is fiercely proud of its identity.

To understand today's parade is to appreciate several thousand years of ceremonial gift and exchange. These small villages have traditionally relied upon trade between remote islands to share scarce resources as well as enlarge the gene pool. Goods were bartered and a cash economy of sorts developed around an item of known worth. In these islands it was a string of carefully honed pieces of pink triton shell, often combined with white shell and black banana seeds. Today's complex and colourful display is not just a 'Thanks for the boat' but also a celebration of exchange between the isolated islands and the representative of the more distant village of *Gavman* (the government).

STARSHIP IS BECALMED. A comprehensive blackness surrounds us, punctuated only by floodlights shining from the tender deck. Clouds of bizarre bugs clatter on the tungsten lamps, mirrored in the silky water beneath by jellyfish and phytoplankton attracted to the glow.

With daylight duties at an end, the crew prepares for a big night out. However we are not slipping into jeans and shirts, but wetsuits and dive tanks. The night life in Milne Bay is not on a dance floor but beneath the water's quiet surface. Loaded with cameras and lights, the team looks like a clandestine force of extra-terrestrials. Odd noises of compressed air, beeping dive computers and high-powered tungsten lamps must register as a close encounter for the bewildered locals assembled on the beach. Or perhaps we just look like dorks.

Joining the line-up on the aft platform, I suck on my regulator and run through last-minute safety checks, feeling decidedly clumsy in gear designed for another world. Weight-belt, BCD uninflated for negative entry, air on. With a single long stride towards the beach we crash hard into the warm water with the elegance of stampeding wildebeest. Our small group of divers is suspended in space, headlamps twinkling, plumes of bubbles rising to the glassy surface. Weightless in the darkness, fellow divers cast yellow wands with torchlight. There's little reference for depth or orientation, save the digits on a glowing LCD screen and a compass.

Strange, colourless organisms float in the water column, propelling themselves by all means of contractions or simple tails. Some, like the box jellyfish, are deadly – so despite the 35°C water we wear long-exposure suits to stop the unseen nasties from touching our skin.

My dive buddy, Enrico, and I sit for a moment on the muddy bottom, torches off, watching the moon shimmering and distorting in our effervescent breath. The water is oily-warm, and the fine sediment of filamentous algae drifts in clouds as we practise the precision art of blowing bubble rings. Our halos wobble skyward in chaos before breaking up completely.

It's another world.

A rubble slope is veiled in an unstable layer of fine algae that supports a complex web of highly evolved animals. These tiny creatures have adapted bizarre appendages or unusual behaviour to secure their survival and represent some the greatest triumphs of evolution in a fiercely competitive ecosystem. We make our way carefully, searching every inch for a close encounter. Progress is slow, methodical and confined to the small area visible within the beam of the lamp. It's like looking for needles in a giant haystack.

Gradually a freak show materialises before me, lurking camouflaged on the bottom or tucked beneath coral heads. A rare and brilliantly coloured harlequin shrimp staggers under the weight of a struggling worm; a pair of enormous eye-like markings on its pincers bluffs predators with a distorted impression of scale. Two blue robotic eyes, each with three pupils, swivel on articulated stalks to survey me. The six-pupilled mantis shrimp gradually shuffles out of hiding on eight legs, the armoured front pair clutched close to the body like a boxer primed to strike. The colourful plankton-collecting feathers of Christmas tree worms wave in the current, only to disappear completely into the coral upon the slightest suspicion of a predator. A shiny leopard-patterned epaulette shark slides under a coral head, its lime-green cat eyes monitoring my approach, then slithers away into the darkness.

My heart rate is slow and breathing carefully measured. A trance of sorts sets in as I hover over my torch in just 5 metres of water. Beneath are the well-disguised eyes of a stargazer. It's a fearsome fish that buries itself beneath the sand, remaining invisible but for its eyes, an array of ragged teeth and a flickering tongue that is used to lure smaller fish. It usually ambushes its bewildered prey, administering a handsome bite. I sit for half an hour vainly waiting to see the damn thing take a fish.

Michael waves his laser-pointer at me from 30 metres away. It's an accessory he recently acquired and has been testing with the blind faith of a gadget-freak. The thing gets my attention and I leave the non-compliant stargazer for a much more interesting engagement. Whether it is technological supremacy, diving prowess or just plain luck, Michael has discovered one of the rarest cephalopods on the planet. So uncommon, in fact, that marine biologists struggle to agree on its classification, and for years it was lumped in with another species altogether.

The mimic octopus looks very ordinary but its behaviour is quite astonishing. It will actually change its form and behaviour to imitate another animal less interesting to a predator. It accurately impersonates a flounder skimming along the bottom, a mantis shrimp perched in its burrow, a sea snake or a firefish – each mimicry carefully

Active page 73
See the crazy critters of the Solomon Sea. Download the video clip.

chosen to disagree with the palate of its assailant. Divers don't come around too often and the poor octopus has a hard time discerning exactly what species we belong to, so it runs through its entire repertoire of mimicry before finally retiring to its hole exhausted.

In shallower water Michael and I come across a round crater marking the abode of a 2-metre bobbit worm. Only its open jaws are displayed at the bottom of the hollow. Iridescence rims an arrangement of fine teeth. As I watch, I can't help but to construct a *Star Wars* analogy: it's something like the massive desert creature that finally swallows Boba Fett in *Return of the Jedi*. Only there's a twist: upon sensing the presence of its prey, this creature can surge upward, seize a fish in midwater and drag it into its hole for consumption. Once again Nature goes one up on Hollywood.

Scuttling over the mucky bottom is a bright-orange boxer crab with a stinging sea anemone gripped in each claw. With no venom of its own, to defend itself the crab dances before a predator threatening a punch from its painful 'gloves'. The relationship is symbiotic because the anemones benefit from the small particles of food dropped by the crab during feeding.

It's encounters with critters like these that make diving in this region so extraordinary. Papua New Guinea is at the epicentre of global marine biodiversity. The number of plants and animals in Indo-Pacific waters, an estimated 1500 to 2000 species, is five times greater than that of the Caribbean. More than 40,000 square kilometres of coral reef supports an ecosystem that is more-or-less intact: there is no developed commercial fishing industry and the small coastal population uses traditional and sustainable fishing methods.

We surface at 11 pm to find 20 or so canoes waiting at the surface. The intrigued occupants have paddled above our video lamps for two hours in wait – one young brat called David has even taken the

Watching bubbles, three young boys from Bunama wait for the *Starship* crew to surface. Some would free dive to meet us 10 metres underwater.

opportunity to scratch his name on the ship. Mary watches as I stagger from the water. She grins under the glow of my headlamp, which illuminates a dental horror and large chunks of thick red betel-nut paste. She came to deliver a taro, and pats it with affection as she hands over the prize. 'Tenk yu tru, Mary,' I slur in my best Tok Pisin. My chin has gone numb and I think I may be dribbling, which would add authenticity to my humble acceptance of food. I offer a couple of pencils in return but she declines in a dignified manner.

I'm a little cold, still wearing fins and 20 kilos of dive equipment. Clutched in my shivering hands are two pencils and a truly awful tuber with the taste and consistency of vinyl glue. It's midnight on the equator. Forty people are staring at me from canoes. How odd.

WILD GUIDE

Papua New Guinea must be one of the most extraordinary places on Earth. The country has colonial ties to both Germany and Australia, but European influence has not diminished the enthusiasm of indigenous Papua New Guineans for their cultural heritage, which is complex and diverse. Hotels cater for tourists wanting to see the main attractions, but off the beaten track few facilities exist. However, the people are friendly and those willing to rough it a little are in for the time of their lives. Port Moresby has a reputation for petty crime so the usual travelling precautions apply. During election time political competition can lead to violence, but this is also the most vibrant time to visit. The best time to visit is during the dry season, March–August. Consider timing a visit to coincide with the Mask Festival, held every July in East New Britain, or the Western Highlands Mount Hagen Culture show in August. Both are raw, colourful displays where locals outnumber tourists a hundred to one.

GETTING THERE

Flights to Papua New Guinea depart daily from Australia, Hong Kong and Tokyo. There are daily flights on Milne Bay Air from Port Moresby to Alotau, the regional capital of Milne Bay province. From there the islands of Milne Bay are accessible by boats such as Rob van der Loos's *Chertan*, which offers a live-

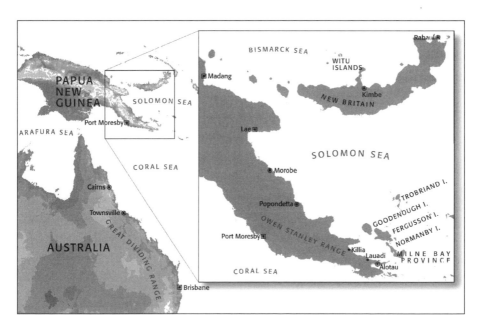

aboard charter with all dive facilities and local guides. Alternatively try your luck and hitch a lift aboard a local cargo boat. It will get to its destination... eventually

CONTACT

Rob van der Loos
MV Chertan Marine Charters
PO Box 176
Alotau
Milne Bay Province
Papua New Guinea
Tel: +675-64 11167
Fax: +675-64 11291
Email: info@chertan.com

FURTHER READING

Rob van der Loos, *Living Reefs of the Indo-Pacific,* Reed New Holland, 2001

Paul Theroux, *The Happy Isles of Oceania: Paddling the Pacific,* Fawcett Books, 1993

Ernest W. Lee et al, *Lonely Planet Pidgin Phrasebook,* Lonely Planet, 1999

WEBSITES

MV Chertan Marine Charters
www.chertan.com
The Nature Conservancy
http://nature.org/wherewework/asiapacific/papuanewguinea/
Undercurrent
www.undercurrent.org/UCnow/dests/PapuaNewGuineaInfo.shtml
World Wide Web Virtual Library
http://coombs.anu.edu.au/SpecialProj/PNG/Index.htm
TANIM (documentary on the Highlands produced by the author)
www.tanim.cc

Following pages *p. 77 (top)* Children fish in the lagoon at Kitava Island in the Trobriand group. Though the rainy season is nearly over, tropical thunderstorms pound the islands most afternoons. *p. 77 (bottom)* Children ingeniously make toy cars from seeds in Walindi, New Britain. (Photo: James Frankham) *p. 78 (top)* The WNB Culture Group, with their wooden hats, are star performers, belting out half a dozen favourites passionately embellished with actions. *p. 78 (bottom)* Damselfish swim through the spines of a spawning radiant sea urchin in Lauadi. Watch out for those spines, they really hurt. (Photo: Brandon Cole) *p. 79* A mantis shrimp ventures from its burrow to investigate the photographer. A strike from the front legs can shatter a dive mask. (Photo: Brandon Cole)

palau, ngulu, yap
MICRONESIA

'IT'S UP TO YOU, mate,' says Trevor with a boyish grin. 'You can stay on the boat and suffer the consequences, or you can jump in and swim across.'

Longitude 0 degrees. It's the first time I've crossed the equator by boat and an initiation of inestimable horror will surely befall me if I stay on board the good ship. The alternative, so kindly offered by Trevor, is to swim across the equator. I bank on the devil I know and leap over the side.

The water is more than 5 kilometres deep, the waves are bigger than they appeared from aboard, and I'm undoubtedly being surveyed from

Left Despite being ravaged by fighting during World War II, the Ngermehaus Islands of the Palau archipelago are now among the most idyllic spots on earth.

beneath by apex-predators. I experience light vertigo and suddenly it seems like onboard initiation would have been a jolly good idea.

Dave has chosen the same fate, and I find comfort in the hope that, given the option, a ravenous shark would pick him over my skinny shanks. We sink our heads into the cobalt Pacific and swim for our lives, Trevor coaching us from the aft platform. He's loving it. Head spinning, choking and gasping, I drag myself with exhausted ineptitude onto the aft platform of *Starship*. In truth I loved it too.

Destination Palau: a remote archipelago in Micronesia, six days' sail north of Papua New Guinea. Trevor eases the throttle back on the big diesel to achieve arrival at first light. Navigating the channel that cuts a crooked path through Palau's treacherous reefs during darkness would be a grave mistake.

Dawn comes bright, yellow light sparkling on the wave crests. The entrance to Malakal Channel is clearly marked. On the port side is the rusting hulk of a fishing vessel that got it wrong. To starboard is another upturned hull, foundered on Ngadarak Reef. In boating terms it's like sticking a head on a stake.

In daylight it's not such a task to make it through – the road is clearly visible, a dark blue ribbon of safe water fringed on both sides by iridescent turquoise shallows. Ahead is the long verdant form of Palau, a network of 300 islands scattered like buttons over a reef system 100 nautical miles long. Each island has been subtly undermined by the rushing currents and resembles a mushroom with a yellow stalk and green jungle-clad top. The collusion of islands affords hundreds of natural anchorages and a generous harbour in the lee of Koror Island – the commercial centre of Palau.

Beneath us are the wrecks of Japanese warships sunk during a massive Allied aerial assault during World War II. The surprise attack was so successful that many of the vessels didn't have time to move, and now some 60 wrecks rest on the muddy bottom, each behind a length of chain with the anchor still firmly set. Helmets litter the decks alongside depth charges and ammunition boxes.

We complete the necessary immigration procedures, refuel, provision, then leave port again with an additional crew member who will guide us through the inner reefs to Palau's blue perimeter.

GUY SADAN wears a sunny yellow T-shirt and a grin that originates deep inside a bulletproof optimism. He left Israel five years ago to escape the conflict, to find himself here, overcompensating in one of the most peaceful places on the planet. Sanguine creases extend from the corners of his eyes as he scans the lagoon ahead. Patches of deep, patches of poisonous shallow, and only one safe route. We are now beyond the protection of the Rock Islands and approaching the reef rim that forms Palau's living perimeter.

Rain patters softly on the deck, the wind dies and the water goes silky. We moor In a pool of deep water and transfer dive bottles, cameras and equipment into the tender for the ride through German Channel to a spot called New Drop Off.

Guy swings me a big, barb-less fishhook on a cord with a snap-shackle on the other end. 'It's a reef hook,' he beams. 'You clip the shackle on here.' He fastens it to my BCD 'I'll show you where to put the other end later.'

Dressed in all the dive-technica with this hook I feel like Batman, ready to swing from skyscrapers through the streets of Gotham City. Guy rolls in first to test the current, surfacing seconds later and spitting out his snorkel. 'Ee's rr-i-i-i-pping!'

We clamber hand over hand down the mooring line, our bubbles not rising but rocketing backward. Four knots of current rumbles over the reef and rushes in my ears. I am puffing heavily, kicking strongly to make headway towards the reef wall where Guy is tucking his reef hook under some old coral. I do the same. The current catches the underside of my body, lifting me off the reef. I am thrown backward and upward with tremendous force until the lanyard pulls me up with a crack. Legs sail behind me like the tail of a kite in a tempest, fins feather, arms flare. I can feel the adrenaline in my fingertips.

The tide roars up the reef wall and we sail on the updraught. It's not a constant flow but comes in almighty gusts, buffeting our bodies and threatening to rip the masks from our faces should we dare to look over our shoulders. A grey reef shark cruises along the wall, with only the faintest movements of its tail and gentle corrections of the pectoral fins. It nonchalantly comes within a couple of metres of us, apparently uninterested. The visibility is some 50 metres and we can count the shapes of 26 sharks patrolling the wall. I feel like I am being displayed before the predators like salami hanging in a deli. We flap in the terrific current with sharks to the left, sharks to the right, above and below. Back on the boat we fizz with excitement. It certainly rates as the most dramatic dive many of us have ever done.

But we don't have time to dwell on the occasion – we have treasure to discover on the island of Yap.

A LONG TIME AGO on an archipelago far far away, there were many villages competing for limited land and resources. On Yap Island, village chiefs struggled for power against competing groups trying to outdo each other building ornate men's houses for unmarried men to hang out in. Like many other cultures of the Pacific, all sorts of commodities were being used as valuables, including shells and turmeric. But that all changed with an exquisite blunder.

A man named Fathaan was a navigator of dubious competence. He departed Yap one day, ostensibly on a fishing trip, and arrived some time later, 300 nautical miles east of where he should be, in Palau.

He would have recognised the error immediately – Palau looks nothing like the low, coralline island of Yap. The geomorphology is of limestone, not found on his home island. Fathaan and his crew were greatly excited with the new material and fashioned some whale shapes from the rock.

Upon returning to Yap, Fathaan was acclaimed as a master navigator and the limestone *rai* (Yapese for 'whale') took on tremendous value as the chief displayed his treasures. They were symbols of a great sea voyage, of daring and mastery of the elements.

It wasn't long before other villages were preparing expeditions to Palau to retrieve limestone. The passage in open canoes was notoriously danger-ous. At the other end prospecting Yapese would have to conduct difficult

Dave and LJ manhandle some Yapese pocket change. The huge *rai* shattered before it could be transported from Palau, and the heartbroken workers abandoned it where it fell. (Photo: James Frankham)

mining operations and at the same time ward off Palauans trying to extradite the invaders from their island. The alternative was to buy the right to quarry the stone through indentured labour for the Palauans.

The whale shape was revised to a more easily carried disc with an oculus at the centre like a giant Japanese coin. The workers could put a heavy piece of timber through the eye of the full-moon shape and carry it across their shoulders. Though the pieces no longer resembled whales they retained the name *rai*. No doubt the irony of the term was not lost on the Yapese porters that dragged the massive, awkward discs through the rainforest. The return voyage was even more treacherous as the vessels were laden with stone discs up to 3.5 metres across and weighing many tonnes.

The value of each coin was assessed by the difficulty of attaining it.

A large *rai* proudly marks a Yap men's house, a building where the ranks of male society meet to politic, tell stories and educate village boys when they come of age.

If the stone was large, if many people had died in the procurement process and if it was of a mineral composition particularly difficult to cut, the *rai* would be considered of great value. The prestige of owning such a coin made the journey worth the hardship – even at the cost of lives.

As I run my hands over the great discs of rock I recreate visions of an ancient people hewing them from the earth. I'm a little confused, a fraction bewildered. It's difficult to animate the static discs with the obligation to community that sent young men on missions that cost their lives. I struggle to get my head around the futility of the process. In the bumps and creases of the crystalline limestone I can feel the marks of the simple stone tools driven by determined hands. These are not coins for trading or simple currency to drive the wheels of a primitive economy; they are monuments to pride. Tokens of great achievement. It's not unlike an athlete enduring years of training to win an Olympic medal, the value of which is more or less negligible. The *rai* are great trophies of solid rock earned by a daring few for the communal esteem of an entire village.

We stand under a brilliant equator sun, a men's house dominating the view. The large coral plinth is studded with posts supporting a sensational gable pointed to the sky in a gesture of obvious aspiration. It is woven with intricate patterns of coconut fibre. Dolphins play in black and white friezes and wooden gulls project, singing, from the soffit.

Lined up along the northerly prospect is an array of stone money, of varying sizes and cuts. The biggest is more than 3 metres in diameter. This is, quite literally, a stone money bank, a graphic example of the communal nature of Pacific Island cultures in which individual wealth is not celebrated. Everyone in the village knows who owns which piece but they are all displayed as common prosperity.

The inherent difficulties of the world's largest currency must have been quickly realised: 'Can I have a loaf of bread?' 'Sure, that will be one three-tonne rock, please.' So the *rai* were used only for ceremonial exchange of big-ticket items: to buy wives, purchase land or offer apologies. The stones themselves were never physically moved – the ownership change was simply committed to village memory. It seems the tiny island of Yap pioneered the global revolution of cashless trading thousands of years before electronic banking was invented.

Certainly David O'Keefe didn't quite understand. He washed ashore in 1878 after being shipwrecked on the reefs. The Irishman was quick to befriend the locals and encouraged them to trade in copra and sea cucumbers with Spanish colonials. However he noticed that the Yapese were far more interested in risking life and limb in pursuit of stone money than in harvesting copra for colonial favours.

So O'Keefe organised expeditions to Palau in large vessels and supplied metal tools from Hong Kong so that the Yapese could extract the treasured *rai* more easily. In exchange they would work on his copra plantations. But he failed to understand that the value of the *rai* depended upon their rarity and the difficulty of extracting them. He returned boatloads of perfectly hewn and finished stone coins to the island but they turned out to be virtually worthless. A smaller rougher piece was of greater value because people had died retrieving it. The currency devalued and there was high inflation, quickly signalling the end to the tradition of collection.

The original stones are of great value today for ceremonial exchange, land transactions and dowries, but increasingly the US dollar is becoming of greater importance.

JEFF IS WEARING yellow shorts and a baggy white T-shirt displaying a large portion of tanned paunch beneath the hem. His hair bears evidence of a massive peroxide spill. He's the kind of joker whose buoyant personality instantly grates, then becomes utterly endearing.

The irrepressible Brit leaps around the tender cracking witty one-liners with a potent enthusiasm then splashes into the green water, arms, legs, flippers pedalling madly. 'Ten minutes! We've got ten minutes!' he calls above the hiss of air purging from his BCD.

Every now and again I have to breathe deeply to nullify the lofty sensation of hyperventilation. Small waves of nervousness and excitement (I've never been able to tell the difference) are brewing in my chest.

We descend through 16 metres behind Jeff's plume of bubbles. The water is littered with fine particles of plankton, the visibility less than 10 metres. The current is ripping. Jeff has chosen to dive in a channel leading right through Yap's fringing reef. It's called Goofnuw, and at this time of the tide, it has a fair volume of water moving through it.

Five divers huddle in an eddy created by a large coral head, sitting on our backsides, legs spreadeagled, reclining on our tanks which are dug into the sand. Enrico is grinning so hard small chains of bubbles are escaping from his corners of his mouth. We must look ridiculous. It's a bit of a change for the *Starship* crew, who have just had 40-odd dives searching meticulously for tiny specks of life in the mud of Papua New Guinea.

This time we sit and wait for a beast that we cannot overlook.

Ten minutes clicks over and Jeff props himself up on the tip of his fins. His calculations of time and tide are right on the money (the blond is from a bottle after all) and he points down the channel. A faint shadow slips silently over the sand. My heart thumps in my ears and my breathing waxes.

The movement is long, lingering, precise. The 4-metre wings describe perfect sinusoidal curves: broad, arched, massive. It could be the most beautiful thing I have ever seen. So this is a manta ray.

Not so many years ago sailors were terrified of such a sight. The 'devil ray' inspired fear, a portent of horror to come. Undoubtedly a giant ray leaping from the water would be a fearsome spectacle. Yet beneath the surface, in the manta's medium, it is awe-inspiring. Spine-tingling.

She rises on the turbulence over the coral, soaring directly overhead, then stalls, suspended above the staghorn, flaring her great wings backward like a skydiver. A thousand fish not bigger than fingers swarm around the manta, penetrating the gills and the mouth, and picking

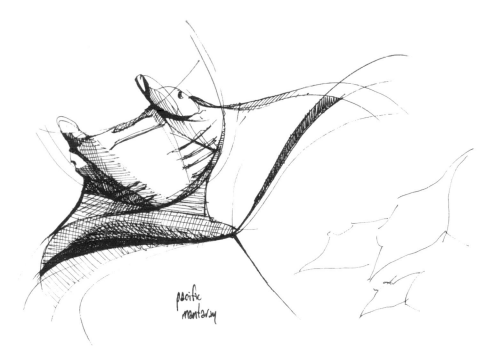

pacific
manta ray

Active page 90
See the mantas of
Yap. Download the
video clip.

parasites from the rippling fuselage. Her left wing twists elegantly and she rolls down-current in a balletic arc, slipping away into the haze. Not a ripple, not a sound. No wake, no disturbance, save the gaping jaws of the *Starship* crew.

Mantas are pelagic, that is to say they are a migratory open-ocean species. But Yap is a remote island surrounded by water more than 8 kilometres deep and the great rays behave more like permanent residents. The dive guides even have names for the individuals that return time and time again. This beauty is called Valerina.

Ten minutes later Valerina returns, this time flanked by two wing-pilots, Blot and Bubbles. Three huge rays pirouette above us, sweeping through a repertoire of manoeuvres that astonish the air-sucking, blundering divers propped up on their tanks like puppets. The sublime and the ridiculous.

Typically *Starship* dives explode on the surface as crew members rush to communicate everything they wanted to say underwater. Sentences, fragmented and scrambled, pour over each other and adjectives fly. But returning to the tender from this dive is utterly different. We're speechless: head shaking, awestruck, fresh out of talk. The communication begins to trickle out on the long ride back to the ship as we piece together what we have seen, finding words, reconstructing what we couldn't comprehend underwater.

Next time I will be better prepared. I will be ready for opening bars of the symphony, for the beating of wings, for the soaring shadows of Yap.

IT'S AN UNUSUAL immigration procedure on Ngulu atoll. With a total population of just 17, Ngulans don't muck around with bureau-cracy; basically you saunter ashore and ask the chief if it's OK that you're there.

It's a nice change for Captain Trevor, who usually rolls out the red carpet for officials who fill out meaningless forms, stamp this, that and the next thing, inspect everything from refrigerators to underwear drawers and occasionally ask for bribes to ensure that 'everything goes smoothly'. This time he just has to run us ashore in the tender.

A long coral reef extends 50 metres out from a white beach overhung by coconut palms. Turquoise waves beat against the shore and a breeze rattles in the trees. A group of women shelter from the sun beneath a blue plastic canopy and weave flax baskets, their fingers moving many times faster than their bodies. After a short while it becomes evident that only two are actually doing anything. The remainder are children and older women reclining against the privileges of their age.

You could walk clear across the main island in 15 minutes. Tracks criss-cross shaded clearings and we wander towards the centre – which seems like the best place to go when you start at the edge. Traditional huts are clustered together in groups of four or five, representing extended family units. Great care has been taken to sculpt gardens around each hut, with coral blocks and beaten-earth paths networking the cluster. The steep roofs are thatched and walls fabricated from woven palm matting. Floors are elevated to allow air to circulate underneath.

Sixteen-year-old Fabian takes great pleasure in giving us a tour of his house. It doesn't take too long because you can see the inside from the outside. The width coincides exactly with his height and it is a couple of times his reclined length with a high-gabled roof. He's even got a pot plant. He escorts us across the atoll to meet the chief, warning us that he might be sleeping.

Four large green turtles lie flapping on the coral. A joker in a black T-shirt rolling a cigarette nods at us.

'Ummm…Hi.'

He nods.

'Are you the chief?'

He flicks his head in the direction of the longhouse.

'Thanks.'

The longhouse is a modern building in contrast to the thatch-roofed houses. It has a concrete floor, concrete walls with louvred windows and a well-reinforced tin roof. It looks like it could withstand a hurricane. Indeed it has to, as the 4-metre-high atoll is frequently buffeted by cyclones and this building serves as the emergency shelter for the Ngulans. From here Fabian can peer out of the rattling windows and watch his less-robust dwelling get washed into the Pacific.

Sprawled on the sturdy floor is a lightly clad gentleman who must be the chief. Actually 'lightly clad' is a generous expression for a man wearing jandals and a loose sumo-style lap-lap. He is asleep, and from what the man in the black T-shirt is trying to tell us, pretty well tanked too.

So we pull up a block of coral and sit down, waiting for the chiefly stupor to wear off. About an hour later he staggers from the shelter rubbing his eyes, looks at the five white guys assembled on his island and picks up a lengthy steel tube.

At this point I begin to wonder just how simple the immigration procedure will be.

Michael (who always seems to operate in a realm of exquisite good luck) takes the initiative and stands up, taking care to respect the rules

Chief Mike is flat out on Ngulu atoll.

we learnt in Melanesia – always treat a chief with the highest degree of respect and never assume a position that is physically higher than them.

'My name is Michael...' he begins. And the chief bursts into a smile.

'My name is Michael too, but people call me Mike.' We all are a little relieved and chuckle along nervously.

Chief Mike nods at project director Michael's tactful request. 'No problem,' he says, apparently quite charmed by the engagement, then gets on with his day.

Today is a very big day. There are two boats in the lagoon, the most crowded it has been since World War II. The Federated States of Micronesia patrol boat is a grey number with a dozen guys in lap-laps sleeping on the deck. As we approached in the tender earlier the captain was so formal as to throw on his uniform shirt and do up a button or two. The boat visits Ngulu once every couple of months and drops off the post – an occasion much anticipated on the island and cause for a bi-monthly hoe-down with a celebratory turtle feast. Hence the flapping beasts capsized on the coral before us.

Mike lurches over to the closest turtle, fastens a rudimentary noose around its head and drags it over a larger piece of coral. He picks up the steel tube, swings big and brings it down on the head of the turtle with a jaw-thundering wallop. It's pretty hard to watch: man beating living daylights out of endangered species. But this is how it has been for several thousand years of indigenous habitation in Micronesia. A couple of turtles a month is sustainable.

The other turtles, inverted and flapping, watch on as Mike makes his first incision through the neck, just above the plastron. With little ado he slides his arm though the opening up to the shoulder and, with a look of intense concentration, rummages around in the interior. The organs are removed one by one and Mike proudly displays each before dropping the bloody goodies into freshly woven flax bags.

'This the heart, this one,' he beams as if suddenly struck by the beauty of life. 'See, it's still moving.'

After Mike extracts the eggs and the entrails, children take to the task of cooking as he nods off again. Palm fronds are dumped rather unceremoniously on top of the carcass and it is set on fire. Orange flames dance triumphantly above the flippers, which remain raised in final surrender. I am struck by the brutality. And by the simplicity.

Climbing back into the tender I notice a lump of polystyrene, a drowned jandal and sheet of orange plastic – the washed-up wreckage of consumerism. I feel embarrassed. Plastic bottles and product packaging are so easily discarded and are just so jolly durable. Jandals must have a half-life of several thousand years.

The effects of global warming are similarly far-reaching. Some clown drives his 4.5-litre SUV down the road to pick up burgers for dinner, and half a world away the people of Ngulu are wondering why their reef is dying and why they are have more devastating cyclones more frequently, when they're doing the same things they've always done.

Nine of the ten hottest years ever recorded occurred between 1990 and 2000. Continued accumulation of greenhouse gases is expected to lead to rising temperatures, more severe weather events, increased ecosystem stresses, shifting precipitation patterns, increased ranges of infectious diseases, coastal flooding, and other impacts that we are only beginning to understand.

I tuck the plastic into the forward locker of the tender and pretend it didn't happen. Just like some governments are judging the cost of reducing emissions too great. And pretending like the ozone hole doesn't exist or supporting all sorts of fringe conjecture that the planet isn't warming, that weather patterns aren't changing, and that they shouldn't have to change either.

WILD GUIDE

PALAU

The blue-water diving in Palau is second to none. It is not unusual to have 20 sharks within eyeshot, and that can be as far as 70 metres. Because Palau is a massive seamount in very deep water there are plenty of large pelagic species, including oceanic sharks, mantas, tuna and billfish. People are friendly, speak English and use US dollars. Most visitors to Palau arrive on Continental Micronesia Airlines, with regular flights from Guam. There are daily connections to Guam from Tokyo, USA and other metropolitan centres. Two weekly flights from Manila and two charter flights from Taipei currently connect Palau directly with other metropolitan Asian cities.

CONTACT

Navot Bornovski
Fish 'N Fins
PO Box 142
Koror
Republic of Palau 96940
Tel. +680-488 2637
Fax: +680-488 5418
Email: fishnfin@palaunet.com

PHILIPPINE SEA

YAP

FEDERATED STATES OF MICRONESIA

Yap Trench
▼ - 8527m

NGULU

Palau Trench
▼ - 8054m

PALAU

Koror ▣

PACIFIC OCEAN

PHILIPPINE SEA

Jayapura ▣

BISMARCK SEA

PAPUA
NEW
GUINEA

SOLOMON SEA

INDONESIA

ARAFURA SEA

Port Moresby ▣

CORAL SEA

YAP

There are two main entry points to Yap – Manila and Guam. For Europeans and Asians, Manila is the most common hub, flying via Palau. For travellers from Japan, Taiwan, Australia and the Americas, you fly through Guam. If flying from Guam you can book a ticket to Palau with a free stopover in Yap. The Manila–Palau–Yap route is the shortest, but it's only available on Wednesdays.

CONTACT

Manta Ray Bay Hotel
PO Box MR
Yap 96943
Federated States of Micronesia
Tel: +691-350 2300
Fax: +691-350 4567
Email: yapdivers@mantaray.com

NGULU

If Ngulu is neglected by the world, it's for good reason. It's very hard to get there. About the only chance you have is to talk your way aboard the Federated States of Micronesia patrol boat that drops off the mail every two months. People who visit this way will be allowed to spend a day on the island but I expect you would have to be very nice to Mike to be allowed to stay longer – because 'longer' comes in multiples of two months. And forget about ringing home if you get stuck, there isn't a phone.

WEBSITES

Palau Visitors Authority
    www.visit-palau.com
Fish 'N Fins Palau
    www.fishnfins.com
Yap Divers / Manta Ray Bay Hotel
    www.mantaray.com

FURTHER READING

Neil Levy, *Micronesia Handbook*, Moon
    Travel Handbooks, Emeryville, 1999
Clyman Otis, *Adventures in Yap*,
    Vantage Press, 1994
Michael Parfit, 'Islands of the Pacific',
    National Geographic, March 2003

Following pages *p. 97 (top)* Within Palau's fringing reef is the Seventy Islands Wildlife Preserve. The islands are protected by World Heritage classification and no one may land. *p. 97 (bottom)* Chief Mike disembowels a green turtle – with its lippers still flipping – removing enough eggs to fill a palm basket. *pp. 98–9* Children fish with spears in the shallows of Yap Island's lagoon.

komodo island
INDONESIA

IN THE 1954 cult classic *Godzilla*, a 20,000-tonne radioactive lizard wreaks havoc in the streets of Tokyo, ripping trains apart and trampling innocent people – until Dr Serizawa uses his oxygen destroyer gun to kill the beast. Director Ishiro Honda could think of nothing more frightening than a giant lizard on a rampage. And so effective was the recipe that it gave birth to the modern teeth and claws genre of horror.

Or maybe it began earlier than that. Peter Pan's greatest fear was the Captain Hook's ticking reptile and I remember the tale of Sir Lancelot, the knight in shining armour with a mighty sword, who succeeded in slaying the dragon that terrorised innocent villages and destroyed

Left Portrait of a monster: a Komodo dragon drools at the prospect of devouring a chicken.

their crops. I think he won a fair maiden for his troubles.

Harvard sociologist E. O. Wilson contends that we're not just afraid of predators, 'we're transfixed by them, prone to weave stories and fables and chatter endlessly about them, because fascination creates preparedness, and preparedness, survival. In a deeply tribal sense, we love our monsters.' Scaly and menacing, dragon-like creatures have populated our most potent images of horror. And today I will discover why. *Starship* is anchored in the crook of Toro Lawi Bay, a deep elbow on the eastern coast of Komodo Island. I sit on the aft deck thumbing through pages of material that have just fallen from a satellite into the fax machine.

Indonesia represents one of the most biologically diverse regions on earth, harbouring many endemic species, and it has been identified by the WWF as a global conservation priority area. Komodo Island has one species that is unique. So notorious in fact, that it has stolen the name of the island. Komodo's dragon is what we have come to see. Pixilated images on the fax depict a meat-eating goliath 3 metres in length. The articles use words like 'beast', 'monster', 'bloodthirsty', and include superlative descriptions of size. I am strangely fascinated.

Lieutenant van Steyn van Hensbroek of the Dutch colonial administration was similarly struck in 1910. I can imagine him kicking back in a smoky Javanese establishment and swapping stories of daring crusades in the East Indies with his compatriots of the Dutch pearling fleet. But he couldn't top their tale of 6-metre-long 'land crocodiles' on Komodo. When he made it to the island he found he couldn't top the story because the fishermen had stretched the truth a little. However he did manage to bag a 2.1-metre dragon and sent the skin and a photo to the director of the zoological museum in Java. The zoologist didn't share the facility for overstatement that typified his pearl-fishing countrymen, and he reported to the world simply that van Hensbroek 'had received information…[that] on the island of Komodo occurred a *Varanus* species of unusual size'.

Unusual size indeed. The largest recorded dragon weighed 66 kilograms and was 3.13 metres in length. Like van Hensbroek, I have to see this for myself.

*

THE OCHRE HILLS sheltering the bay seem remote, barren, even vacant. They are creased like a crumpled quilt with shadows cast by the rising sun, elongated silhouettes of tamarind trees make bizarre faces on the sunburnt grass. It doesn't seem like the kind of place that would harbour a monster. Not this morning; it's too pretty, too quiet, altogether too innocent for carnivorous lizards.

The *Starship* crew climbs a rickety wooden ladder onto the wharf and swings up bags of gear. This time we have packed infrared equipment to operate the cameras remotely, because one doesn't get too close to a Komodo: its bite is as mean as its bark. There are more than 50 strains of bacteria in the saliva, at least seven of which are highly septic. And not 'highly septic' like scratch-on-your-knee going-pink; 'highly septic' like one-bite-and-you're-dead-in-a-couple-of-days.

Jusuf Yenata waits patiently at the ranger station. He wears a giant blue cap emblazoned with a gold park emblem and holds an iron-wood stick with a fork shape at one end. Underneath the copious hat is a forever-young Indonesian countenance – a face that hasn't changed an iota since his fifteenth birthday. Peter Pan with his flimsy stick is our sole defence against the dragon.

I guess I expected Sir Lancelot.

Jusuf grins sheepishly.

The dragons live on just three islands in Indonesia, declared a World Heritage site and Man and Biosphere Reserve by UNESCO in 1986. Komodo National Park protects both terrestrial and marine species over an area of nearly

Jusuf Yenata and his ironwood stick

2000 square kilometres. It sits on the Ring of Fire, at the junction of the Sunda and Sahel tectonic plates. Volcanic eruptions created the first land here during the Jurassic period some 130 million years ago. At that time land bridges connected many of Indonesia's 18,000 islands, allowing the dispersal of terrestrial flora and fauna, including ancestors of the Komodo dragon.

In the nineteenth century, zoologist Alfred Wallace drew a famous line on a map of the Pacific, showing the divide between bird species that typified either Asia or Australasia. In doing so he defined the most important basis for theorising migration patterns. Though the world knew little of tectonic plates, Wallace's line had accurately described the edge of the Sundan shelf, connected to continental Asia. Komodo National Park sits within the fuzzy ink-blot of the line and hosts an unusual range of animals representing species from both Asian and Australasian ecological regions. Wallace had stumbled upon evidence underlying the most important geological theory, and the most controversial theory of the origin of species, on the very same day. However it was Charles Darwin who received the kudos with some nifty publication of academic papers.

Dappled light falls on a leafy path winding between the lontar palms. The web of an enormous golden orb spider shines. The air is dry and smells of sweet tamarind fruit and long-tailed macaque monkeys crash through the treetops.

Jusuf skips ahead, scanning the brush for the dragon.

The scrub is deep, dense, impenetrable and yellow like spun gold. The majority of terrestrial plant species on Komodo can obtain and retain water. Fire-adapted grasses thrive. Robust root systems allow quick rejuvenation and seed dispersal is wind-assisted, colonising burnt areas over a great distance.

The tell-tale swoosh mark of a Komodo tail traces a serrated line across the dusty track and into the grasses of a clearing.

I can almost hear Bach's Toccata and Fugue in D minor echoing between the trees. In 1938 English adventurer Pat Collins brought his gramophone to Komodo, ostensibly to test the response of the dragons to acoustic stimuli. He wandered into the bush, surrounded himself with man-eating lizards and played a handful of favourite tunes. However after frequent Bach recitals and Handel's Largo at great volume, Collins concluded that the dragons were insensitive to music.

But it appears now that Collins's taste in music was the problem. It fell outside the dragon's restricted hearing range. Had DJ Pat cranked out some tail-tapping beats between about 400 and 2000 Hertz, the dragons may well have whistled along.

Eyes darting from side to side, Jusuf scans the surrounding grass for signs of movement. His ironwood stick in his left hand, he touches the knife on his belt with his right. Despite guiding in the Komodo National Park for many years, our Peter Pan maintains a healthy fear of the giant lizards that inhabit the island.

The Komodo dragon is an ambush specialist and can easily out-run the most enthusiastic human over a short distance. Typically they prey on deer, but they also eat pigs, water buffalo, horses, long-tailed macaques, dogs, goats, sea turtles, bird eggs and even other dragons. It is not unusual for adults to devour their young. The dragons will prey on humans as well. The most famous case was that of Mr Baron in 1974. He was a Swiss tourist who lagged behind his group. All the rescuers found was his camera.

Grass crackles at the edge of the clearing. 'Auas, auas, be careful!' calls Jusuf, who dances in front of the cameras, stick waving. Through the grass I can make out a long low form. It could be a log, a pile of stones – anything but a 2.5-metre lizard. Basking in the morning sunlight, the dragon rests almost completely obscured, warming its scaly skin. Its forked tongue tests the air in syncopated stabs. Dark glassy eyes monitor the surrounds, filmy eyelids switching over the corneas from back to front in a disturbing fashion.

And the smell! I had not considered for a moment that the most impressive feature of a 3-metre lizard would be the bouquet. Eau de Rotten Meat just won't be a big seller at the fragrance counters this Christmas. It's repugnant. The oral bacteria factories and a predilection for carrion are responsible. But consider for a moment that the olfactory sense of *Varanus komodoensis* is sensitive enough to detect meat from as far away as 4 kilometres. One can only imagine the stench they perceive.

Dragons are not at their best in the morning. Their blood is cold, metabolism low and instincts soft. But give them an inch and they'll take a mile, so we keep our distance. Snout held high, its forked tongue stabbing the breeze, the ancient reptile saunters into the clearing. Cameras clatter and videotape rolls. The guest of honour has arrived.

The skin is khaki in coloration, textured like the chain mail of a medieval warrior, and painted with dust. Breath whistles through its body. Four muscular legs prop up a robust fuselage like the buttresses of a tremendous cathedral. The tail is a couple of times thicker than my leg and continues in a serrated ridge to meet the base of the flat head. Its lips twist into an evil smile.

I wouldn't trust him as far as I could throw him. And by my estimation it would be less than six inches.

A Komodo dragon nicknamed Mister Auas patrols the beach in search of food. The tongue makes contact with the Jacobson's organs, analysers that 'smell' food by recognising airborne molecules.

We cautiously follow the dragon along leafy tracks and gradually become adept at gauging the critical distance between camera and quarry. I make half a dozen attempts at getting the dragon to walk over the camera. Each requires guessing the path of the beast and swiftly burying the unit a couple of centimetres to match the ground clearance of a Komodo – also guessed. All things considered there's a few too many degrees of estimation involved. The reptile gets side-tracked or takes an alternative route, or I simply forget to press the record button in my haste to leave the track of a faster-than-expected dragon.

However on one section of the track I spot a fallen tree and a rocky outcrop. The path is clearly defined on each side by dense brush. Michael comes running around the corner, cameras and packs swinging from his shoulders. 'Hurry up! He's coming.' Images of frightened public running for their lives from *Godzilla* flutter in my mind as the rest of the *Starship* crew dash past wide eyed.

My fingers turn to thumbs as I buzz down the exposure a couple of clicks and make a hasty white-balance. Roll…and before the tape touches the video head I'm legging it north with the remote in my mouth.

The dragon, this time, has gathered its stage presence and strides right over the lens, which tracks down the full length of the body before being knocked over by the vacillating tail. It's a small triumph for tiny cameras.

And cut; that's a wrap. Thank you, Godzilla.

THE 1400 PEOPLE of Komodo village have learnt to live with the monster in their midst. *Ora* – as dragons are known to locals – take goats, dogs and chickens and sometimes enter family homes for rats and fish. But even when the reptiles steal bones from the graves of their ancestors, the people of Komodo village do not defend themselves. The *ora* is the fabric of their legends. Some even worship it as a higher being. It is a complex response from a people under constant threat.

A line of houses on stilts stretches along the beach as if washed ashore in a great storm. The rusty iron roofs look at peace beneath the bronze hills. Outriggered sampan fishing boats with cryptic Indonesian names

Boys play in Toro Lawi Bay while one of their companions is dying from a
dragon attack. Locals have learnt to live with the constant threat.

are awaiting the rising tide and the fishing sorties of nightfall. Two young
boys in coloured sarongs off-load supplies.

Hery sits on the knee of his father in a simple corrugated-iron dwelling.
The 11-year-old's eyes are deep, dark and morose. A soul trembles behind
speechless lips.

Hery was bitten by a dragon just outside his village of Kampung
Komodo a few months ago while collecting bark from the forest. Though
his friends drove the beast away with stones, and the doctors at Labuan
Bajo Hospital stopped the bleeding, Hery is growing increasingly weak.

Typically dragons ambush their prey from the undergrowth and
administer a toxic bite. The victim often escapes but the Komodo simply
follows, waiting for the sepsis to creep through the bloodstream. In a few
days the prey is too weak to run, too tired to fight, and the shadowy
stalker will move in for the kill. The immune system that protects the
dragons from their own toxins remains a mystery still under research.

It is just a matter of time until the bacteria destroys Hery. He hasn't spoken a word since the attack. His father explains that the dragon 'tore away his soul'. The words seem to epitomise the relationship between man and monster here on Komodo. The *ora* is feared and revered, hated and idolised, but so much a part of the society that destroying the threat is never considered.

With these thoughts in mind we join Jusuf back in the bush. A Komodo has captured a wild boar and it's our opportunity to film a dragon doing what a dragon does best. Tearing at the belly, it rips open the abdomen, consuming the intestines in gulps. It is so intent on its meal that it pays little attention to the quiet chaos around it. DJ scrawls notes for the German journal on a wad of Post-it notes and swaps facts with Lou, who is writing for the English site. Jan interviews Jusuf for *Stern*, Europe's biggest weekly news magazine. Two photographers peer through long lenses, eyeballing the feeding lizard, waiting for a break in the hard afternoon light.

Fine grey dust fills my lungs and sticks to the edges of my eyes. Grit grinds in the zoom ring of the camera lens. Yesterday a lizard licked this camera and I spent all afternoon disinfecting it – I'm now paranoid about touching the body. We've been standing under the equator sun for hours and we're beginning to lose concentration just when we need it most. The dragons will seek shade during the hot mid-afternoon, but they are warm and fast. Now is not a good time to loiter in long grass.

'Komodo!' calls one of the rangers.

We redistribute quickly as another enormous male crashes through the undergrowth on the opposite side of the clearing. Jusuf tugs at the collar of my shirt. 'Careful, this could be fighting.' He fends off the approaching dragon with an adroit poke of his stick.

With a burst of speed the dragon slams into the other feeding individual, pressing his full weight on its back. This Komodo is particularly aggressive and is known by the rangers as Mister Auas, literally translated as Mister Be Careful. He has a reputation for throwing his weight around.

Behind the lens I am taut with adrenaline.

The dragons seem to agree on mutual gusto and abandon the conflict

Two Komodo dragons make short work of a large boar. After consuming the intestines they rip the animal in two and swallow the pieces whole.

in favour of the food. Heaving at opposite ends of the dismembered porker, the lizards rip it in two, one swallowing the prized head in a single gulp. Komodos have an intramandibular hinge that lets their jaws open unusually wide, allowing them to bolt their food whole. They are capable of consuming 80 per cent of their body weight at one sitting; this was a mere snack.

The forked tongues are out again, tasting the air for another feed, blood still shining wet on their snouts. This afternoon the lizards have shown their true dragon colours: bloodthirsty, powerful, aggressive, poisonous. The speed with which a Komodo can shred and consume an animal is disturbing. Beneath the scaly exterior, their blood runs cold. The reptilian instinct that stimulates them to plunder the intestines of a live creature is so far removed from my own motivations that it scares me.

But the dragons should be more fearful of humans. Since the Indonesian economy crashed, residents of the remote islands of Indonesia have been forced to find a livelihood where they can. A daring band

Active page 111
Watch a Komodo swallow a pig whole. Download the video clip.

of rustlers from the neighbouring island of Sumbawa regularly braves a treacherous strait crossing to Komodo Island – as well as the jaws of sleeping dragons – to poach deer and water buffalo from the national park. A single kilogram of this meat fetches 30,000 rupiah (about US$3.50), double the average daily income of Indonesians.

And as the natural prey of the dragons is pilfered, so the carrying capacity of the island decreases. Gradually the dragons are becoming a fairytale of their own.

TORO LAWI BAY twinkles in the darkness. Hundreds of fishermen have put to sea in their *banca* canoes rigged with kerosene lamps to attract the catch. Squid swarm to the surface, chasing the pools of golden light. The fishermen lift the *bagan* nets that hang beneath the outriggers and scoop buckets of slimy cephalopods into the canoe. There are few sounds save the putter of well-worn engines and the mutter of Indonesian spoken between fishermen. Twists of pearly smoke from clove cigarettes, backlit by the lamps, rise in the darkness.

The invention of the outrigger canoe in Indonesia occurred around 5000 years ago and was as revolutionary as the wheel was to land-locked people. It opened up the possibility of trade between the thousands of islands in an archipelago spread over 3.1 million square kilometres of water. The canoes also allowed more widespread settlement; approximately 6000 of the islands are now inhabited.

The waters of this region have been tropical for the past 100 million years. Adaptation has filled the smallest ecological niches with bizarre creatures found nowhere else on earth. New fish and marine invertebrate species are discovered on a regular basis. These habitats harbour a thousand species of fish, more than 250 species of reef-building coral and 70 species of sponges, not to forget the dugong, sharks, manta rays, dolphins, sea turtles and at least 14 species of whale. The upwelling of nutrient-rich cold water along the southern extremities of the archipelago contributes greatly to the abundance of life in the region. In fact scientists believe that the reefs of Komodo are some of the most productive in the world. Coral reefs, mangroves, seagrass beds, seamounts and semi-enclosed bays with ripping currents ensure variety of habitats.

But an increasing human presence within Komodo National Park is putting a strain on natural resources. The population has risen more than 1000 per cent since 1930 and is now well over the carrying capacity of the area. Demand for televisions, radios, boats, buildings and pilgrimages to Mecca has increased with outside influence, putting more pressure on the fisheries that 97 per cent of the local community rely upon as their main source of income. And fishermen will go to great lengths to increase their catch…

BOOM! THE EXPLOSION sends shockwaves through my body and I gasp on my regulator, then exhale hard in a flurry of bubbles. Context is blurred; this is the sound of a mid-city construction site, not a richly decorated reef wall 25 metres underwater. Another boom resonates through the water, bones rattle and my frightened eyes meet Trevor's.

Unmistakable. Blast fishing.

We are diving off the island of Moyo, not far from Komodo National

komodo village

Park. Out here there is no one to police illegal fishing methods, and fishermen regularly add bombs to their tackle box. The practice was introduced to the Indonesian Archipelago in World War II as an easy way to catch schooling reef fish. Bombs made from chemical fertilisers, pesticides and old ammunition are dropped from canoes. The blast stuns the fish, which are collected by divers. Five square metres of reef can be destroyed with a small charge, representing one of the most destructive anthropogenic threats to coral reef ecosystems anywhere in South-east Asia.

The damage is indiscriminate. Not only are preferred species and sizes killed, but also fish and marine invertebrates that are commercially unattractive. The reef is completely destroyed and takes more than 25 years to regenerate. In the worst cases there is so much coral rubble that polyps will never reseed. To compound the damage, demolishing the habitats of reef-dwelling fish also diminishes the food source of larger open-water species. The shockwaves of blast fishing are felt through the entire ecosystem.

Indonesia is also the largest supplier for South-east Asia's live fish trade. Cheap cyanide is used in a diluted form to stun reef fish. The coral is smashed to extract the poisoned fish, which are then packed in ice and shipped to Hong Kong. There they are revitalised to live in restaurant aquariums from which customers choose their lunch. The mortality rate of the captured fish is high and the coral that isn't smashed to bits is poisoned by the cyanide, overgrown by filamentous algae and eroded away. It will never support another reef system.

Blast fishing, cyanide poisoning, reef gleaning and the use of pesticides and traps are now the greatest threats to the ecosystem. Sadly, these methods also destroy alternative income generators like eco-tourism. Amongst the locals awareness of the problem has increased, but outside the park this has had little effect on the behaviour of a population living at subsistence level.

THE LOFTY SPIRES of Komodo glisten gold and hopeful in the failing light. Giant fruit bats hang inverted from the twisted branches of mangroves, shrieking. As the sky darkens and eerie shadows deepen on the hillsides, the bats rise on translucent wings and fly east in their thousands to the neighbouring island of Flores to feed.

Komodo is haunted. Haunted by bats, haunted by reptilian monsters. And haunted by men.

Already as much as 52 per cent of the reefs in and around Komodo National Park have been damaged. But today the local Balai Taman Nasional Komodo and the Nature Conservancy, a United States-based environmental organisation, are working together to protect the park's biodiversity and educate the locals. The results have been dramatic. Patrols have reduced bombing within the park by 80 per cent. Surface treatments applied to bombed reefs have also proved successful in regenerating the coral. Local staff trained for the monitoring tasks are now training new staff to expand the management of the park. And seaweed aquaculture and pelagic fisheries have been developed as alternatives to destructive fishing.

Though Lancelot's blazing sword may slay a dragon, I'm not sure it could combat the brigade of blast fishermen. Not even Dr Serizawa's oxygen destroyer gun could protect the reefs from poisoners. The champions of our folklore cannot leap to the assistance of this place. And their mythical weapons are of no consequence here. It's real-life heroes that will ensure the protection of the park – Jusuf will save Komodo with his ironwood stick.

WILD GUIDE

While all-inclusive tours to Komodo National Park can be organised from Bali, it is cheaper to go from Labuan Bajo, on Flores Island. Here there are touts on the main road selling tours to Komodo and Rinca Islands – both of which have dragons. If you can get a group of 4 to 6 together you'll only pay around US$20 for a couple of days. A note for female travellers: it is not wise to go to Komodo if you have your period.

GETTING THERE

Merpati Air flies from Denpasar, Bali, to Labuan Bajo six days a week for around US$150 per person round trip.

CONTACT

Komodo National Park Head Office
(Balai Taman Nasional Komodo)
Labuan Bajo
Flores Barat
NTT 86554
Indonesia
Tel: +62-385-41004, 41005
Fax: +62-385-41006
Email: tnkomodo@indosat.net.id

FURTHER READING

James B. Murphy et al, *Komodo Dragons: Biology and Conservation*, Smithsonian Institution Press, 2002

Claudio Ciofi, 'The Komodo Dragon', *Scientific American*, March 1999
David Attenborough, *Zoo Quest for a Dragon*, Oxford University Press, 1986

WEBSITES

Komodo National Park
  www.komodonationalpark.org
Komodo Dragon Central
  www.isidore-of-seville.com/komodo/
Woodland Park Zoo
  www.zoo.org/komodo
Merpati Air
  www.merpati.co.id

Following pages *p. 117 (top)* Even water buffalo, the largest land mammals in the park, are prey for big Komodo dragons. *p. 117 (bottom)* The hills of Toro Lawi Bay. *p. 118 (top)* This video camera, placed in the path of an advancing Komodo, had to be thoroughly disinfected. *p. 118 (bottom)* Large mammalian carnivores like lions leave a quarter of their kill unconsumed, but Komodos eat far more efficiently, forsaking only about 12 percent of the prey. They eat bones, hooves and hide. *p. 119* Using small cameras operated by infrared remotes we could get close to the Komodo dragons relatively safely.

kalimantan
INDONESIA

A MUTED LIGHT presses through the hazy air of Kumai and the river slides past, skirted by dense rainforest. The sun plays on the hulls of small sampan canoes and dances in their wakes. My traveller's appetite begins to stir.

An insubstantial wharf supports cranes raised in anticipation like antennae. The cargo vessels rafted up alongside have the characteristic Indonesian high bow, the double-ended hull and an accommodation unit teetering like an afterthought over the stern. Logs are piled high in the deep hulls awaiting transport to foreign ports. Small speedboats, customised with stickers, dodge debris in the glassy water of the Sungai

Left One of the lucky ones, an infant orang-utan clings to the arm of its mother at Camp Leakey in Tanjung Puting National Park.

Kumai. More boats clutter the refuelling dock and a bedraggled pump attendant puffs on a clove cigarette as he fills a jerry can.

The dusty streets are like those of any frontier town in Indonesia. Mopeds travel in swarms, competing for pavement space with pedestrians who perform daring feats of self-preservation. The buildings are organic in construction, expanding, dividing and multiplying in response to the changing need of the occupants.

Kumai has undergone a massive transformation in the last decade. The once-smoky frontier town is now a rapidly expanding centre of the timber trade. The screaming chainsaws that frantically mill the Indonesian hardwood so sought after in the West have cut clean through Kumai's society. The industry promises riches for those who dare to creep in shadows: the great majority of the trade is from illegal logging inside national park boundaries. Kumai is consuming itself.

We shuffle through the noisy streets asking for a guy known only as Andi. People know people, and pretty soon we're face to face with the man. Three years ago Andi left his nomadic Dayak tribe in Borneo's hinterland and walked out of the jungle to seek work in burgeoning Kumai. His knowledge of wildlife and a new understanding of English set him up well to be a park guide.

Andi is a soft-spoken guy with a stubbly moustache, cropped black hair and pearly Indonesian skin. Side-stepping flying motorcycles he explains the catastrophe of Kalimantan. The Indonesian part of Borneo is in the grip of some of the most extensive deforestation on earth. Logging and gold mining are stripping the region of trees and pressure from environmental organisations is only accelerating the pace of deforestation – the timber syndicates want to extract the logs while they still can. The logging has penetrated Tanjung Puting National Park, which contains some of the last commercially valuable timber. It is predicted that at the current rate of deforestation, lowland dry forests will disappear from Kalimantan by 2010.

The park's 400,000 hectares of tropical heath forest, mangrove and peat swamp is hard to police and about 40 per cent of it has been damaged by logging and forest fires. It's no small band of clandestine loggers –

5000 people are illegally logging in the park and 7000 illegally mining for gold. Those who stand to profit are not the tree fellers, who are paid a pittance, but the powerful timber bosses.

The problem is not specific to Kalimantan. Loggers have invaded almost all of Indonesia's remaining forests, including protected areas. Tropical forests are in serious decline worldwide. In the 1990s, 152 million hectares of natural tropical forest were lost, a dizzying figure of 8.7 per cent of the total tropical forest worldwide. And as the forest disappears, the natural habitat of hundreds of species goes with it. One of the most tragic stories is the dwindling population of orang-utans. Kalimantan is one of only three places in the world where these great apes are still found in the wild. In 1998 there were only 2000 in Tanjung Puting National Park, the largest 'protected' area of swamp forest in South-east Asia and certainly the only protected habitat of the orang-utan.

STARSHIP'S 6-METRE TENDER cuts through the water, throwing spray wide in great orange arches as we head up Sungai Sekonyer, one of the tributaries that leads into the heart of the park. The sun is still low in the sky, silhouetting the rainforest on each bank. Carving to the left and right Andi guides us to Tanjung Harapan, the first park station on the river.

The station is a small collection of huts with a floating dock supporting several semi-buoyant craft. High in a tree ranger Erwin wears an orange headband, a wiry goatee and armfuls of baby orang-utans. He is teaching them how to climb – this rehabilitation centre prepares young orang-utans for reintroduction to the wild. Many have been orphaned as a result of deforestation, or sold as exotic pets.

The youngest orang-utan is a fiery fellow named Adung. At only ten months old he is already showing his intelligence, recognising his own image in the LCD display on the video camera. He grips the display in one hand and the lens hood in the other, and rocks back and forth watching his own picture. His arms are long and extraordinarily powerful, and Adung appears to be equally dexterous with both hands and feet, right-side-up or upside-down.

Just last week Erwin found Lady in a nearby village, locked in a cage.

She is two and a half years old but has never learnt to climb. So today he lifts her into a small tree outside the centre and encourages her to hold the branches and move around. She looks decidedly weak and struggles to coordinate herself.

'They have lost their instincts and they fear the jungle,' explains Erwin, 'so we have to teach them how to climb, to find fruit and how to make a nest.'

Like humans, orang-utans have social mechanisms for coping with the stress of orphanhood. A pair of four-month-old orang-utans at Harapan never leave each other's embrace. There is always one arm around the other, even when feeding, as if holding on to the only constant in their lives. It's sad and beautiful at the same time.

Since Dr Birute Galdikas founded the rehabilitation centre in 1971, 283 orang-utans have been set free into the jungle. The work is impressive, but one wonders whether she and her colleagues can keep up with Kumai's chainsaws.

It is demand that creates supply. And the culpability for the homeless orang-utans lies squarely on the buyers of snooker cues, picture frames and furniture, or those who prefer to sleep on futon beds. It is hunger for tropical hardwoods in developed nations that supplies fuel for the chainsaws and wages for the loggers in Indonesia. Japan, USA, Europe and increasingly China are the most voracious consumers of tropical timber in the world. And it is estimated that 60 per cent – nearly 1 million cubic metres of timber per year – of the tropical hardwood entering the United Kingdom is illegal. It's ironic that some of these nations are the ones campaigning the hardest for habitat protection.

Erwin scrubs at the head of young Adung. Covered with foam, he drags on Erwin's T-shirt and wipes the water from his grimacing face. He knocks over the bucket, saturating the ranger. The orang-utans are washed on a daily basis with antibacterial soap and Dettol to protect them from infections transmitted by their human keepers. It seems as much of a

Left A ranger at Tanjung Harapan gives Adung an anti-bacterial bath. Necessary contact with humans during rehabilitation exposes the young orang-utans to disease.

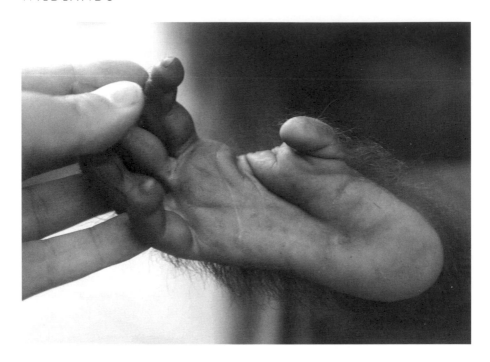

Orang-utans are the largest tree-dwelling mammals in the world but these feet have never learnt to climb. Rangers hope to reintroduce captive orang-utans to the wild.

trial for young Adung as any infant undergoing a good scrub-down. He clings furiously to Erwin's arm with eyes scrunched up tight and spits water from his lips. Eventually the ranger has to transfer the desperate primate to his leg so he can use two hands to wash.

Leaving Erwin with his soapy subject, we continue up-river for another 10 nautical miles to Pondok Tanjung, the next park station. Running upright down the dock, his long arms extended outward for balance, is a gibbon called Michael. He has become somewhat of a local identity at the station. He leaps the 4-metre gap between the dock and the boat and dances around the pontoons, searching for food. We hear a *zip* as he opens the cooler and extracts a can of Coke with pride. Fortunately the ring-pull eludes him.

But the apples do not. Michael sits on the radar arch of the tender trying to get his teeth around the awkwardly large apple, chewing loudly with his mouth open. He sports a white beard like a wise old man but his energetic amber eyes constantly move. He finally abandons the half-finished apple and sets to chewing a sticker off my tripod. I wonder how long he will have 'Made in Italy' stuck to his teeth.

With dusk falling we join Mr Emang in his houseboat. Smoke rises from Andi's clove cigarette as our host dishes up nasi goreng beneath the eerie-green incandescence of a Coleman lamp. Stretching out on the roof, we listen to the jungle come alive. I've never heard sounds like this before. Great whoops and shrill whistles. Bleeps and croaks, clicks, crackles and twitters. It's captivating.

Throwing a MiniDisc recorder and condenser microphone into my pocket I trundle off along the walkway, waving to the rangers enjoying their tea in Pondok Tanjung hut. There is enough light from the moon to see on the walkway, but the rainforest is as dark as the inside of a cow. I shuffle along the narrow track that we walked so briskly in the afternoon, until I am surrounded by the cryptic tunes of the night. It is a purely sonic experience. My eyes register nothing at all.

I record about 40 seconds of sublime audio. And then experience pure fear – unsolicited, unannounced, invisible. A huge snort erupts from the bush a few metres ahead. Adrenaline explodes into my arteries and I spin on my heels, running for my life through the blackness.

Blind panic. Animal flight.

After a couple of metres the beast stops the chase. I sit alone in the glow of the ranger station to recompose my shattered constitution. I'm panting like a lunatic, my hair is standing on end and my body quivers.

Back at the houseboat the crew finds my breathless story hilarious. They giggle at the audio of a snort and a rush of feet. There is nothing that reveals what it was that chased me, or even comes close to documenting the terror I felt. Perhaps it was a boar or maybe some undescribed and hideous jungle creature. I don't intend to investigate.

A tangible blackness descends, quickly followed by the nagging whine of mosquitoes. Malaria is rife in swampy river deltas and we dash for the protection of mosquito nets, but it takes a while to fall asleep on the roof of Mr Emang's little painted boat. I'm tired, and relatively comfortable, but the encounter with my most primitive instincts keeps my heart racing all night.

MORNING ARRIVES and so does the curious gibbon, who finds his way in where the bugs could not and rolls on the sleeping bags until we can ignore him no longer.

Only concentric rings formed by water dripping from the mighty rainforest canopy disturb the surface of the Sekonyer. Light presses through the broad leaves like the stained-glass windows of an immense cathedral. The river here is a rich brown, evidence of the mining operations farther up. There is concern that mercury used to extract gold from the ore since 1990 leaches into the water and according to locals there are fewer fish and crocodiles in the Sekonyer. There are even reports of abnormalities in the human population living on the river. In 1999 the Indonesian Institute for Science found extremely high levels of mercury – but the results were not released publicly.

Andi leads us up-river in the tender.

As we make our way deeper into the park the river slithers before us like a serpent. The jungle becomes denser and the radio hisses with static as we leave communication range. Strange frogs and unidentified birds whistle alien tunes from the bush. Tiny tributaries – often occupied by a pole house, a wild arrangement of elevated platforms linked with ladders and gabled roofs of palm fibre – split off the main channel.

Turning hard to starboard into one tributary, we pass the police station. Orangutan Foundation

International funded the building in the hope that the presence of police would deter would-be illegal loggers and miners. Our wake turns gold with the brackish water. Now, more than 40 kilometres inland, the jungle closes in on both sides and we slow to a crawl. Perfect reflections of the trees are mirrored on the surface.

A 20-metre-high observation tower marks the dock of Camp Leakey. A long finger wharf extends 100 metres over marshy grasses into the heart of the camp. Here Birute Galdikas and her associates have logged over 100,000 observation hours of orang-utans.

The great apes often wander freely between the ranger accommodations but today we have to head into the forest. We don't have to walk far.

There is a crash in the vegetation above and a large female descends to the forest floor. I set the camera on the tripod and pan to follow. Unyuk is an orang-utan with a reputation for destruction and has a crazy look in her eye. We retreat quickly.

I have left cameras in the path of all sorts of animals, from Komodo dragons to white rhinos and sharks. Often it is an effective way to capture close-up material without disturbing the animal. So I do the same this time without a second thought. The second thought occurs a few moments later: maybe orang-utans are more curious than lizards.

Unyuk snaps up the video camera and mimics my movements, panning and tilting while watching the LCD display. She holds the camera where I held it and as I held it. One could be forgiven for thinking she was simply a very hairy film-maker. But she soon abandons her media career in favour of demolition work and sets to dismantling the device, stripping off the accessories like a service technician with a grudge.

One cannot take something from a possessive orang-utan without risking an arm, so instead we try to entice her away, even breaking the golden rule and offering food as she rips off the wide-angle lens. I feel like an absolute idiot. Eventually we recover the camera and run back to camp with a measure more respect for the intelligence and strength of the orang-utan.

*

RAIN PATTERS on the corrugated-iron roof of the shelter. Pattering turns to hammering and we scramble to pack the camera gear away from the rapidly increasing humidity. An inch of water covers the ground in minutes. Thunder rolls ominously.

The downpour ceases as quickly as it started and the surface water slinks away. We can hear crashes in the canopy on all sides. The forest is alive with orang-utans. The air rumbles with the call of a king. Kosasi has arrived. He is an enormous male weighing more than 150 kilograms and nobody messes with Kosasi. As the dominant male he can mate any female he pleases. When he is present no other male will be seen for fear of death. His authority is absolute and his authority is unchallenged.

Andi whispers some timely advice: 'Never get too close. Never block his path, and if he charges…run very fast.'

When Kosasi stands upright we almost look eye-to-eye, yet the breadth of his shoulders must be twice mine. His arms and back are muscular, his body squat, powerful and covered with coarse red hair. Massive cheek pads hang on each side of his face and air sacs in his throat create a thunderous *woop-woop* call that silences all the females and sends the males running for cover. He carries the presence of a mafia godfather. Intimidation personified. Two years ago the rangers needed to weigh and measure Kosasi and shot him with a tranquilliser from a Dayak blowpipe. To this day the only thing that will subdue a hostile Kosasi is the display of the pipe.

Orang-utans prefer to feed alone and occupy a home range of some 1.5 square kilometres each. But as the forest is cleared the orang-utans increasingly look for protection close to the park stations. In a smaller area there is greater competition and rangers are forced to distribute food.

Extensive forest fires in 1997 and 1998 further reduced the habitat of the orang-utan. Indonesian authorities estimated that the total area affected was 520,000 hectares. However this figure was based on reports by palm-oil plantation owners, who were responsible for much of the fire setting. Using satellite data and ground checks the

Active page 130
Hear the song of the king. Download an mp3 of Kosasi's call.

Loggers take timber from inside the national park boundary. Over 70 per cent of Indonesia's log production is derived from illegal sources like this.

German-supported Integrated Forest Fires Management Project put the figure at closer to 5.2 million hectares in 1998 alone – ten times the official figure. The Ministry of Forestry and Estate Crops never made the new data public, citing the need to 'protect national stability'.

The problem is that illegal logging is a multibillion dollar industry and the profiteers are willing to use a little muscle to shimmy the logs out of the country. Opposition to regulation is strong within towns like Kumai, which depend on logging and palm plantations for income. Locals demonstrated against the staff of Orangutan Foundation International after it cooperated with police to remove illegal loggers from the park, and burnt down the offices.

So strong is this resistance that the foundation's Dr Abdul Muin fears for his safety. 'They destroyed our office. No files, no documents, we lose everything. And the staff houses were also robbed.' He looks desolate. 'I don't know what to do.' There is a strong undercurrent of fear in the once-peaceful port of Kumai, and law-abiding citizens find it difficult to avoid being part of the lawlessness. 'It's a very complicated problem,' continues Muin. 'People do not respect the authorities here any more.'

While stringent laws require permission to cut, transport, process and export timber, they are simply not enforced, through either lack of resources or the complicity of officials. Forestry ministers and high-brass government officials seem more interested in lining their pockets with generous stipends from logging barons than protecting endangered species.

The former Minister of Forests Marzuki Usman did manage to reduce logging in April 2001 by placing a moratorium on the cutting and trading of the sought-after tropical timber ramin. He also listed the species on the Convention on International Trade in Endangered Species appendix with a zero quota, making import into foreign countries at least as difficult as export from Indonesia. However the timber bosses now ship the logs through neighbouring Malaysia, 'legalising' it as Malaysian timber with fraudulent paperwork and consigning it through the ports of Singapore, China and Japan.

To work in Tanjung Puting National Park NGOs must be sycophantic to the authorities. Aggressive condemnation of the regime is out of the question. But is the softly, softly approach to protecting this critical biome doing more harm than good? Surely trying to rehabilitate juvenile orang-utans whose habitat is being rapidly annihilated, at the same time as attempting to stay on-side with those responsible for its destruction, is ultimately futile.

Though he is already an orphan, young Adung can be considered lucky. He has found safety in the care of park rangers and his immediate future is promising. However the odds are stacked against others of his kind. Many believe that the rainforest and its inhabitants will remain for less than a decade without urgent government intervention. The fight will continue until the last stand of trees falls.

BACK ON *STARSHIP* we begin the long journey down the Sungai Kumai and back into the Java Sea. Out of earshot of the chainsaws the forest seems peaceful again. Sullen. The river slithers past, burdened with the flotsam of civilisation, carrying the venom of mining and logging out to sea. With the slag and sawdust go the hopes for the survival of an ecosystem.

This is toxic water for *Starship*, and not because of the mining. There are more than 100 acts of piracy reported by commercial shipping companies every year, and a third of them happen in Indonesian waters. Some involve common robbery at anchor and some vessels are attacked at sea. Some are hijacked, their crew killed or despatched in liferafts.

Every week we download a report from the International Maritime Bureau to gauge when and where pirates are most active. There were three attacks here last week. Five fast boats attacked a gas-supply ship near Sumatra, but the assailants were fended off with fire hoses. The same thing happened to another vessel the day before. And earlier this week a tug and barge were hijacked. The fate of the eight crew remains unknown, as does the whereabouts of the vessels.

The situation is compounded for *Starship*. Our exact position is broadcast on the internet, along with details of the vessel, crew and the vast haul of electronics held on board. They could bring a shopping list. We have been briefed on how to avoid or evade pirates, and in these waters we try to travel in daylight. When night passages are necessary we stay more than 5 nautical miles from the coast and avoid known hotspots altogether, always keeping a close eye on the radar for suspicious vessels. The threat adds a degree of intensity to every night watch.

For much of the course to Singapore the depth doesn't get much greater than 30 metres, a reminder that this region once used to be above sea level and, many archaeologists contend, densely populated until worldwide flooding events between 8000 and 14,000 years ago. Ahead is the Strait of Malacca, a channel between Sumatra and mainland Malaysia with a huge concentration of commercial shipping traffic. But beyond the gauntlet of pirates and commercial shipping is a massive expanse of Indian Ocean. Crossing it will take more than two weeks: eight days to the Maldives where we will refuel and provision, then a further six to the Seychelles. My bunk rumbles with the thrum of *Starship*'s V8, pounding away 24 hours a day behind my cabin wall. But if I press my ear against the hull I can hear the rush of salt water, the restlessness of travel.

Sometimes it feels like we're always on the go, never resting or taking time to dig very deep into the heart of a culture. But there's value in seeing the world an inch deep and a mile wide. Few people have had the opportunity to intensively document 60 countries in three years and it allows a unique perspective. A thousand days isn't very long to circumnavigate the earth, so one day in three must be spent on passage to cover the 75,000 nautical miles. Nine nautical miles in an hour; 3000 nautical miles across the Indian Ocean. We are on our way, Java water curling off the bow, onwards, to Africa.

WILD GUIDE

Tanjung Puting National Park is a sinking ship, a titanic ecosystem on the verge of ecological collapse. If you want to go, I suggest you do so right away, because, more than any other location in this book, Kalimantan has a gravely uncertain futre. All-inclusive packages to visit the orang-utans are available with a simple search on the internet. Choose carefully, because while some donate a great proportion of their profits to rehabilitation projects, others are simply money-spinners. The more adventurous can save some money by making their own way to Kumai and bargaining with locals. Mr Emeng and his friend Mr Rani

run boat trips into the national park. The trip can last for one day or three, but an overnight stay is a must if you want to take in the whole environment.

GETTING THERE
Flights to Pangkalanbun airport in Kalimantan are readily available from Djakarta, Kuala Lumpur and Denpasar. A bus will take you to Kumai.

CONTACTS
Mr Emeng
Tel: +62-532-61743
Fax: +62-532-61223

Andi (no surname, he doesn't need one)
Jl. Hm. Idris RT06
Kumai Hulu 582
Kobar-Kalimantan Tengah
Indonesia 74181

Andi has no phone, but you can call his uncle on +62-532-61 606. Contact him or talk to park authorities in Kumai to arrange to see the orang-utans.

FURTHER READING
Louise Barrett and Robin Dunbar, *Cousins: Our Primate Relatives*, BBC Consumer Publishing, 2000
Dr Birute M. F. Galdikas and Dr Gary L. Shapiro, *A Guidebook to Tanjung Puting National Park*, Gramedia Pustaka Utama, 1994
Kal Muller, *Kalimantan: Indonesian Borneo*, Tuttle, 2001
Dave Currey et al, 'Timber Trafficking: Illegal Logging in Indonesia, South-East Asia and International Consumption of Illegally-Sourced Timber', Environmental Investigation Agency, 2001

WEBSITES
Orangutan Foundation International
    www.orangutan.org
Forest Watch
    www.globalforestwatch.org
International Maritime Bureau Piracy Reporting Centre
    www.iccwbo.org/ccs
    menu_imb_piracy.asp

Following pages *p. 137 (top)* Kosasi, the king, enjoys a moment of quiet meditation. *p. 137 (bottom)* Michael the gibbon takes a break from munching on my lunch. *pp. 138–9* A mother comforts her child at Camp Leakey as chainsaws whine in the distance.

aldabra
SEYCHELLES

IT LOOKS AS THOUGH a bulldozer has struggled out of the water and up the beach. Great tread marks tear up the sand. Brian counts, 'Four,' and makes a short note on his ledger. An even number of fresh tracks means all the turtles that came to lay eggs on the beach during the night also left during the night. 'Keep going.' We power on to the next beach of 18 we will monitor this morning.

Brian squints into the hard morning light, and checking, rechecking, his eyes light up.

'Seven tracks,' he issues.

The snout of the tender eases onto the white coralline beach and the

Left A juvenile hawksbill turtle flutters through the shallows of Aldabra's lagoon. Rangers tag and weigh this species to understand why their numbers are declining.

crew leap out as the motors whirr in reverse against the swell.

The remote atoll of Aldabra, marooned in the Indian Ocean between the main group of Seychelles islands and Madagascar, is critical to the survival of the endangered green turtle. More than 2500 nest here every year, and we are here to witness a miracle.

Rangers Brian and Anna lead the way up the beach. By the gauge of the bulldozer tracks I would guess the turtle that rode up this beach last night to have a flipper-to-flipper dimension of some 1.5 metres. Between the tread marks is the smooth track of the breastplate, heaved up the incline against friction, gravity and the laws of motion.

We follow the tracks into the loose sand above the high tide mark. Stuck beneath a stubborn branch of a coastal shrub is an enormous,

Green turtles nest about every three years, laying three to five clutches of 120 eggs each. Statistically, only one in 80 will survive.

exhausted, flapping female. She flounders hopelessly, looking for all the world like she should never have left the water. It's more than a little surprising that these incredible creatures ever managed to slip through the natural selection filter. Grit clings to her eyes and, panting, she rests her head in the sand.

Brian fights with the tree, extending a measuring tape along the carapace and reciting the dimension to Anna, who notes the figures in a field notebook. 'Tag number 4695, length of carapace 115.8 centimetres.' Brian pulls back the shrub and the green turtle lifts her head and inches forward towards the sea, propelling herself on land as she does in water. The surf rolls up to meet her, riding white over her shell. A couple more pushes and she surges into her natural environment, moving as if she was made for it. I follow the shadow with my eyes, knowing that she will be back again to lay in a matter of days.

This is not a pretty place. It has beauty but it is powerful and danger-ous. Empty tortoise carapaces huddle on the razor-sharp coral beneath leafless trees bleached white in the sun. The sky seems bigger and bluer than anywhere else on earth. There is no shadow, no shelter. But for months aboard the ship it has been cited as 'the place I'm really looking forward to'. And *Starship* is a full boat on this leg of the voyage. There are two sponsors visiting the project and a journalist/photographer team from *Stern*, Europe's largest weekly news magazine.

TO BE PERMITTED to visit this remote outpost of science we had to leap through dozens of bureaucratic hoops in Seychelles. Eventually we petitioned the chairman of the Seychelles Islands Foundation. Maurice Loustau-Lallane leant back in his chair, wary of 'boaties' and all too well informed on their impact on the fragile island habitat. 'What do you want to go there for?' he asked in a way that ruled out all but the most sensational reply.

Aldabra is the world's largest and most remote atoll. There is little soil, practically no fresh water, no guano, no phosphate, no deep-water anchorage. The jagged coral can quickly tear shoes to ribbons. It is one of the most inhospitable places on earth. And therein lies its value to science. Over the centuries Aldabra has proved unattractive to sailors, fishermen, settlers and traders. No other Indian Ocean island has been spared human interference for so long. The colony of birds, insects, plants, coral reefs, fish as well as 113,000 giant tortoises has survived as part of a unique and undistorted ecosystem.

A contingent of just 11 people runs the research station. There is no airstrip and nearly 200 nautical miles of open ocean to the closest one. There is no phone, no doctor, no television; only the flimsy longwaves of an HF radio bridge the distance to civilisation and assistance. The nearest hospital is 700 nautical miles away. In fact, the arrival of the *Starship* crew has nearly doubled the population of Aldabra and, it seems, also defused some lurking internal tensions.

The odd community of rangers, scientists and engineers that runs the research station comes under the leadership of an eccentric old gentleman called Louis Ferney Prea. Once he was a sergeant in the British army stationed in North Africa. But now at 67 years of age Louis is separated from his wife and children and has retired to Aldabra, where he administers the lonely project. In his pocket are the keys for the store where the beer is kept. Every ranger, boat driver and mechanic is allowed three bottles a day. Six on weekends. Louis admits to loneliness. And late at night, after his third beer, will even admit to dreaming of naked girls in the lagoon.

There are only two women on the atoll, and one is married. The other is Anna, the tantalising Swedish research officer. Louis teases her and Anna feels like the eyes of the men are constantly on her. But she was brought here to work so she puts her discomfort to one side. She writes what she sees, constantly recording, monitoring, testing, measuring the mechanism that makes Aldabra tick.

Aldabran politics are intricate and absorbing. Sometimes, when tensions run high and the isolation and the heat and mind-numbing boredom penetrate too deep, there are arguments between the staff. And here, in this tiny community visited once in a blue moon by a supply ship, the smallest irritations can tear people apart.

This is the first time on the voyage that I have encountered a situation

biscuit.

as socially demanding as living together on a small ship. All the *Starship* crew know first hand how difficult relationships can become in a closed environment. Relationships with family and friends back home can also be compromised: time and distance, and too much of both.

Brian had a girlfriend back in the Seychelles capital city of Victoria, but she got sick of waiting and ended the relationship last year. 'All day I think about women,' he complains. 'It's making me crazy.' Yet despite the lack of nightlife, the 25-year-old prefers to stay where he is – on the world's most remote atoll with a 60-year-old tortoise called Biscuit that struggles to cover 10 metres in five minutes. Brian has lived on Aldabra for four years.

THE ANCIENT MERCURY outboard coughs, splutters then dies altogether. Slopping around in the wind chop, rangers Steven and Brian work quickly to replace spark plugs and purge the carburettor of water. Black-tip sharks circle in the shallows. The water in the huge lagoon is dropping rapidly

Juvenile black-tip sharks are common in Aldabra's vast lagoon. They feed on hatchling turtles, squid and small fish.

with the outgoing tide and a stranding would be like being dropped in the middle of a desert.

The magical-sounding name of Aldabra is thought to have come from the Arabic word for green, *alkhadra*, because the atoll's lagoon is so large that its colour changes the hue of the clouds above it. Arab navigators taking goods from the African coast north-east towards the great markets of the Indian subcontinent used it as a beacon. Another theory suggests that it owes its name to *Al-dabaran*, five stars in the Taurus group, the brightest of which were used by Arab navigators.

After a frenzy of false starts the motor bursts into life like a frightened animal and the crowd cheers. We steam onwards to anchor in the lee of Grande Terre, the largest island of the four islands in the atoll ring. Packs and equipment are transferred to a smaller tinny that Steven drives like a madman. He wears a pink life-jacket, a baby-blue bandanna and silver Arnet sunglasses. His brow is furrowed and his eyes blink in the wind.

We blast across the bay, waves hammering against the hull. Shockwaves make my cheeks wobble, and I try smiling or bracing my jaw with a multitude of unusual expressions but all efforts are ineffective to prevent the relentless smackering.

Bat-like frigatebirds wheel overhead. Typically they don't collect their own food, preferring instead to scavenge from other birds. To attract the attention of females during courtship the males sport on their throats a red balloon the size of a watermelon. Upon securing a mate the glossy feature shrivels up and disappears.

A flooded mangrove system lies ahead and we weave with small margin for error between coral heads. The water turns a rich brown and an eagle ray coasts past, its caudal fin cutting the surface like a knife. Tangled mangrove roots lace both sides of the tributary. The outboard is jacked up to the second notch and we sit on the bow, salt water lapping over the gunwales.

It takes 20 minutes to reach the drop-off point, where we don packs and feel the weight of the bottled water we are carrying for the first time. Five litres per person per day. That's 10 kilograms each, on top of cooking equipment, food and camera gear. Our feet sink deep into the aerated mud, sending bubbles to the surface around the whelk shells. The trekkers smirk in juvenile amusement at the ridiculous sucking noises made with every step.

An ancient reef rises above the mire, recognisable coral species fossilised into a moonscape. The way to the camp is marked with yellow paint blobs, and reaching each one is a small success. The heat is scorching and we guzzle water frenetically. Small rock pools hold brackish water, each with half a dozen turtles wallowing. One watches me watching him, eyes blinking in turn. I could swear he is winking at the camera.

An hour and a half into the hike we leave behind the grassy wasteland and enter a group of pandanus trees. The distant roar of the ocean indicates we are getting close. As we rise over a final sunburnt slope we see a thin blue horizon and, before it, a tiny hut. Stumbling over the last few metres we reach Cinq Cases.

The shiny aluminium shelter is 5 metres square, walled on three sides with the fourth completely open. Six wooden bunks, with five mattresses, dominate the interior. A pantry of sorts huddles in the corner. The floor is sand. A cooking area with an extraordinarily uncomfortable improvised hammock is propped up on the northern aspect. Roof water is collected in a blue drum via a rough assemblage of guttering and plastic Coke bottles. But it doesn't look like it's rained in aeons.

A dawdle of tortoises presses together in the shadow of the hut, their shells screeching. 'It's rude to stare,' says Lou to one particularly intrigued reptile. He's about the size and shape of a rugby ball and, unperturbed, continues to gawk at the hut's new inhabitants.

Chelonia, the family to which both tortoises and turtles belong, evolved some 180 million years ago when herbivorous reptiles dominated many environments. Ultimately they were replaced by carnivorous mammals on the mainland and survived only on remote islands. Aldabra's tortoises arrived 125,000 years ago, after the last emergence of

During the midday heat tortoises seek the shade of trees, as they are unable to regulate their own body temperatures.

the atoll from the sea. It is believed they floated over the ocean from Madagascar, by virtue of their waterproof exoskeleton and the ability of cold-blooded animals to survive long periods without food. Female tortoises can store sperm for many months in their oviducts, making it possible that just one female washed ashore.

Aldabra is the only ecosystem in the world where the dominant herbivore is a reptile – a living museum that closely represents palaeo-ecosystems of several hundred million years ago. By investigating how the tortoises relate to other animals and plants on the atoll, it may be possible to suggest why the giant reptiles of prehistory disappeared.

Steven cleans a fish for dinner. Brian dishes up some spam. Alan gets the fire crackling and I film a scorpion that scuttles across the sand, pincers extended as if reaching out desperately for some poor sod to grab.

The little corrugated-iron hut positively shimmers in the sunset. Plumes of smoke rise twisting into the darkening sky. An enormous African sun sets over the pandanus palms and a kettle is put over the open fire. Attracted to the heat, a robber crab scuttles out of hiding. Feelers dance. *Birgus latro* is the largest terrestrial arthropod in the world and can measure a metre between leg-tips. The claws are powerful enough to break open the top of a rotting coconut. It will eat almost any organic material, including pandanus foliage, tortoise faeces and its own moulted exoskeleton. There is even evidence of cannibalism. Like their smaller hermit crab cousins, juveniles seek the protection of sea shells. The adults are big enough to avoid predation by birds and live in burrows, emerging after dusk to feed.

Just before midnight we leave the fire to trudge the length of beaches 37, 38 and 39 in search of nesting turtles. The rangers' lights pierce the darkness in fine filaments ending in a glowing patch of golden sand. The prevailing south-westerly is loud in my ears. The night is black as pitch and in the torchlight I feel almost weightless, floating in a cavernous black void.

Only one turtle is discovered. She flaps hopelessly in the coral and Steven repatriates her to the water. Up until 1997 these three beaches were popular nesting grounds for green turtles, but weather patterns have changed and the sand has eroded. Now vast stretches of the beach are nothing more than raw coral. Naturally this poses a problem for the turtles that have been returning to this spot for years.

Up at the high-tide mark I discover a jandal. Another. And another. In fact as far as a torch beam will penetrate there are jandals, hundreds of them in every colour, size and style you can imagine – and not a pair to be seen. Carried by equatorial currents, gyres and trade winds the colourful flotsam must have covered thousands of nautical miles of ocean to make a landing on a remote corner of the world's wildest atoll.

Practising my newly acquired wildlife monitoring skills I run a quick transect along one stretch of beach: 30 in 20 metres. Given this data there should be around 4500 jandals on Aldabra; though behaviour and breeding patterns are unknown their home range is surely extensive and the population seems to be multiplying rapidly.

I finally locate two jandals of similar size with the straps intact. One is basic royal blue and the other green with an unusual mottled pattern on the sole. The research officer grants permission (this is a World Heritage site after all) for me to keep them as a souvenir on the grounds they are an introduced species.

We set off the next morning as the first rays of sunlight warm the land. The starting point of Coco transect is marked with a large zero of yellow paint on a piece of coral and stretches in a straight line for 1.5 kilometres to a coconut palm with 30 markers, each 50 metres apart. Every tortoise within 4 metres of the transect must be measured and sexed and every 200 metres the ranger has to wait for four minutes counting and recording each bird that whistles.

It's an exacting process that must be completed before 9 am. Information has been painstakingly recorded in this way since 1971. The Aldabran giant tortoise can live for 150 years, so a programme lasting several decades is necessary for its life cycle to be fully understood. To date more than 100 scientists from seven countries have invested 50 person-years of research, creating a foundation upon which all future research can be based.

*

BRIAN BRACES HIMSELF against the bowline, arm extended, index finger pointing in the direction of a shadow fluttering through the shallow waters of the lagoon. Steven hunches over the outboard and twists the throttle. The small boat lurches in the direction of Brian's extended arm and the fluttering form darts back to the left. Steven swings hard to follow, misjudges slightly and we crash headlong into the mangroves, knocking the bow-riders from their perch. Steven smirks, Anna scowls and Brian makes some under-the-breath reference to the relative brain sizes of turtle and boatman.

On the next attempt Steven is right on the money. Brian leaps from the bow and at speed crashes into the water on top of his target. The ranger rises from the lagoon with a juvenile hawksbill turtle and a grin from ear to ear. Who said being a scientist was boring?

The exercise is known as the 'turtle rodeo' and is the method by which researchers capture young hawksbill turtles for measurement, weighing, tissue sampling and tagging. Two hawksbills have been tagged this

Splash! Brian tackles a shadowy hawksbill turtle.

afternoon with an evil-looking pair of pliers and a tag resembling a giant silver tooth. Tissue samples were carefully taken from the flipper of each for DNA analysis. Numbers E0759 and E0760 have been well documented and if the tags show up again elsewhere, more will be known about the movement of the population.

Fewer than 30 hawksbills each lay four clutches of eggs per season at Aldabra. Elsewhere, away from the protection of a conservation area, they are killed for their striking shells and the meat discarded, as it is poisonous in one-third of specimens. Aldabra is one of the only places in the world that actually have increasing numbers of turtles. The protection of the local population is doubly important, both for its own sake and as a reservoir to restock other populations that have been depleted or even wiped out.

The odds are not in favour of island species. Nearly 90 per cent of bird extinctions in the last 300 years have been island forms. Two-thirds of endangered species exist on islands and flightless species have disappeared from every other island in the Indian Ocean. Almost all Indian Ocean islands are dominated by introduced birds.

Aldabra is utterly miraculous, boasting many distinct species endemic to the atoll. The most famous is the flightless Aldabran rail, the only survivor of several flightless species, such as the dodo, that once inhabited the Indian Ocean region. It is a small, curious bird that can be attracted by tapping two sticks together. The population is now secure, with several thousand accounted for.

Not so fortunate is the Aldabran brush warbler. The last sighting was in September 1983 in virtually impassable terrain on Malabar Island. A quick check back on *Starship* reveals that the IUCN Red List describes this species as 'almost certainly the rarest, most restricted and most highly threatened species of bird in the world'. Before this voyage is over the Aldabran brush warbler will be officially declared extinct. Such tends to be the lot of the critically endangered.

The greatest present threat to the atoll is goats. From an original population introduced a century ago, today around a hundred goats roam the islands, browsing the vegetation heavily. The tortoises suffer

Louis (left) and Steven chat outside the settlement. The research station is visible in the background.

from a lack of shade and ultimately starve. The natural vegetation is well nigh impenetrable for humans, making eradication of the pest difficult. A number of solutions have been proposed, including expert marksmen shooting from helicopters and biological attack.

However a few rogue ungulates is a small problem to deal with compared with the British military. In 1962 the Ministry of Defence commissioned a military survey of Aldabra for a secret airstrip. The base would include a 4500-metre runway, a dam across the main channel to make a harbour for tankers and a road bisecting the lagoon.

When the Royal Society found out about the plans it appealed to the MOD to prevent this ecological disaster. The project was damned in newspaper editorials, international magazines and a BBC documentary. Despite the public outcry, planning for the base went ahead. Aldabra was saved only after the pound was devalued in 1967 and all British military presence east of the Suez ceased. Then in 1982 UNESCO

Active page 154
Out-take: view more
pictures from Aldabra.

acknowledged the significance of the atoll and named it a World Heritage site to ensure its protection in the future.

It is bewildering that such a treasure could come within inches of total destruction. And it is concerning that Aldabra is a relatively rare success for the environmental movement. The world's most significant industrialised nations still place little political emphasis on conservation.

Sitting next to the fire at Cinq Cases I stare up into the silky black sky, searching for the star *Al-dabaran* that may have guided ancient navigators to this atoll. And I wonder whether modern society still steers by universal points of reference – or are we adrift on an immense sea, unable to agree on basic measures to preserve our inherited natural wealth.

Brian lifts off the boiling kettle and stokes the fire. Sparks twist skyward and he smiles, again convinced that he's in the right place. 'I might go back next year,' he concedes. It seems that, much like the Aldabran rail, Brain has been here so long he has forgotten how to fly.

WILD GUIDE

The only easy way to explore Aldabra is an organised dive-charter run by the live-aboard vessel *Indian Ocean Explorer*, which visits Aldabra from March to April and again from October to November. To visit Aldabra privately is another story altogether. Permission must be obtained from the Seychelles Islands Foundation as the atoll is not usually open for visits by the public. SIF Chairman and Deputy Minister for the Environment M. Loustau-Lalanne, will consider applications on scientific merit and value to the region. The process is necessarily arduous and only a few applications are likely to be accepted. The only way to the atoll other than the dive-charter is on the supply vessel. Limited accommodation for staff is provided on the atoll, but again, this will need to be prearranged.

GETTING THERE

Many commercial airlines fly from major centres to Victoria, the capital of the Seychelles. A chartered aircraft can be organised to fly the three and a half hours to Assumption, an atoll close to Aldabra where the *Indian Ocean Explorer* is based.

CONTACTS

Indian Ocean Explorer
Tel: +1-352-401 5678
Email: info@ioexplorer.com

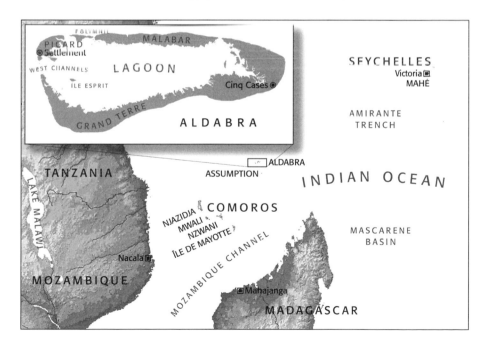

Maurice Loustau-Lalanne
Chairman, Seychelles Islands Foundation
PO Box 853
Victoria
Mahé
Seychelles
Tel: +248-321 735
Fax: +248-324 884
Email: sif@seychelles.net

FURTHER READING
Mohamed Amin et al, *Aldabra: World Heritage Site*, Camerapix,1995
Tony Beamish, *Aldabra Alone*, George Allen & Unwin, 1970
Alberta Seaton et al (editors), *A Focus on Aldabra*, Seychelles Ministry of Education, 1991

WEBSITES
Seychelles Islands Foundation
www.sif.sc
Indian Ocean Explorer
www.ioexplorer.com
UNEP World Conservation Monitoring Centre listing
http://www.wcmc.org.uk/protected_areas/data/wh/aldabra.html
Animal Bytes: Aldabra Tortoise
www.seaworld.org/animal_bytes/aldabra_tortoiseab.html

Following pages *p. 157* Robber crabs have a diverse diet, from hatchling turtles to the toes of hapless passers-by. *pp. 158–9* Aldabra's lagoon is like a slow-beating heart, pumping water in and out of the narrow channels twice a day at a rate of nearly 10 knots.

okavango
BOTSWANA

BARBARA HAS A GRIN that could make flowers bloom. She stands about five feet tall and has a crop of crazy orange hair permed violently, in stark contrast to her pilot's uniform. Fluffy clouds are bundling up on the horizon. Light aircraft squat in formation on the strip like nesting birds. It's 42°C in the shade.

Barbara loads trolley upon trolley of camera gear, tripods, computers and various other outback essentials into the pod of the Cessna. Any single item of our vast array of baggage would be heavier than her. Fortunately Michael's techno-lust is notorious and the airline has booked the equivalent of four seats for him and his digital entourage.

Left Young male lions can be feisty, often breaking away from their matriarchal pride to make a challenge for the leadership of a neighbouring one.

Our pilot mounts a stack of cushions and taxis the rumbling beast to the head of the runway, her nose pressed against the windscreen. With a roar and a gentle ease back on the controls we're in the air.

Below us parched sand veld stretches out towards the fine intersection of sand and sky. Small patches of brush give way to sand dotted with tin-shack settlements and redundant donkeys. Just under the starboard wing an oasis of grass stands out from the brown waste. My jaw drops and the window goes foggy. Lined up along the perimeter of a murky waterhole at the centre are three elephants. Real elephants in the real wilderness. This is my first encounter with Africa's wildlife, and I am overwhelmed.

A million tracks of a million animals criss-cross like haywire stitching and in the distance is the faint green glow of life. Emerald fingers stretch out from sparkling channels. Water is the King Midas of the Okavango Delta – everything it touches turns green. Where there is water, there is life.

The vast Makgadikgadi Super Lake, more than 60,000 square kilometres of water, was once fed by three massive rivers. Seismic faulting rerouted two of the rivers, the lake disappeared, and today only the Okavango feeds the delta. The river flows 1000 kilometres from Angola into the Kalahari Basin, spilling 10 billion cubic metres of water each year into the world's largest inland river delta. Sand carried by the river is deposited in the delta, which is now up to 300 metres deep.

Sedge grass is laid out like a thick green carpet. Small channels and tributaries twist like the coils of a massive silver snake. Red lechwe, striking amber antelopes with spiralling horns, are spooked by the plane and splash their way to safety through the shallow marsh.

Massive tracts of the Okavango Delta have been designated concessions managed by safari companies. Their business relies on a pristine environment and high-value, low-impact tourism like this operation is one of the single greatest environmental initiatives in operation. We touch down gently at Mombo Camp, run by Wilderness Safaris. The organisation has given us an open ticket to their delta operations and over the next week we'll have access to their vehicles and their guides. It's a special relationship; we eat in staff quarters, labour very long hours and work around their guests but are given a little more latitude to explore.

THE LAND ROVER is stock-in-trade for navigating the swamp in these parts. Next to me in the vehicle, Michael has assembled a lens of gigantic proportions. Brooks, our driver, leans against the wheel. He is 24, has been guiding for four years, wears a big 'lucky hat' and has an uncanny ability for spotting small animals at great distances through thick scrub. It must also be noted that he has an unhealthy preoccupation with dung. Many wildlife enthusiasts share this obsession – even Livingstone used petrified hyena doo-doo as chalk. So great is Brooks's fascination with the stinky material that he once left a pile of lion offering on his bedside table for weeks just to see the colour changes it went through.

And now, ankle deep in Kalahari sand, his hands trembling with excitement, he proudly presents a voluminous cake of elephant poo.

Elephants travel in herds of up to several hundred individuals, and maintain some of the most complex social interaction in the animal kingdom.

I am yet to be captured by the dung fixation, and do not particularly aspire to it, but I am curious to discover what Brooks is so enamoured with. So I peer forward, resisting the temptation to breathe, and watch as our guide gleefully breaks the cake in half.

Along with termites, elephants are one of the great elements of the delta formation. Their dung spreads plant seeds over tremendous distances and fertilises the salty, arid soils of new termite-created islands. Elephants also create niches for new species of plant in their vigorous feeding habits.

I nod with a new appreciation for the remarkable specimen in Brooks's hands. He dusts them off with a smile, rams the Landy into first and starts off with a lurch. The vehicle rolls through wide-open plains of yellow grass. We idle over long mounds and around small islands, each with a solitary tree, a termite mound and, usually, a scrawny baboon.

The Okavango is an infinitely complex machine with billions of moving parts, and the itsy-bitsy termite is responsible for more terraforming than any other creature in the ecosystem. Termite mounds in the flat delta sands provide raised platforms safe from the June floods. The mounds are populated by trees and shrubs, which are fertilised by droppings from the animals drawn to them. The islands expand and join others, forming areas that, though barely 5 metres above the water table, are dry year-round.

Brooks points out tiny specks on distant trees. 'Grey loerie…lilac-breasted roller…lesser bee-eater…' The 16-inch tyres grind to an abrupt halt. Brooks stares with intense concentration, as if willing the subject closer. Only after 30 seconds does he lift the binoculars to confirm what his eyes have already told him. 'Mosadi taus,' he mutters, and fires up the Landy to move closer before turning to translate: 'Female lions.'

Six lionesses from the Piaja pride lounge in the shade of a leafy island. The largest of the group is propped up on her forelegs. She stares across the flood plain to a group of Burchell's zebra grazing 400 metres away. One by one the other lionesses sit up to view the distant prospect. Twenty minutes pass, Brooks assuring us that something will happen 'soon, soon'.

The large lioness rolls onto all fours, painted with deliberation. If intensity could be measured, she would teeter off the top of the scale. Her head is low, tail dragging and body in a deep stalk. She advances a few metres at a time, pausing to sit back under the relative cover of grass. After progressing 100 metres, she stops in the shade of a tree. Two of her sisters stalk in sync, advancing when the zebra have their heads down feeding, crouching when they appear wary. In this way they move as far as the leading female but are displaced to the left by some 50 metres.

A herd of Cape buffalo feeds behind the zebra, forcing them a little closer to the waiting hunters. Behind a stand of large acacias loom the heads of three giraffes. It's one of those incredible Okavango scenes: four species in one shot. Five including us. The lions lie motionless – the giraffes are sure to see them and raise the alarm. But the lanky Africans seem more interested in the Land Rover and eventually pass by.

The zebra are relaxed, too far to windward to smell the lions and too absorbed in feeding to see them. The second lion, without any communication with the other two but somehow in concert with both, stalks forward again 100 metres to the cover of a small island. She is on point; the large female and her sister are 100 metres back, on each wing. This is a typical attack formation. After some analysis the large female refines the strategy, trotting around behind an island and disappearing from view only to appear again outflanking the zebra on the right wing.

The bases are loaded. Play ball!

The large lioness surges forward from the right flank. The second lioness starts her run at the same time. The third doesn't move. Zebra raise their heads and scatter in chaos. Muddy divots fly off hoofs. The second lioness is too far back to get involved and drops to the ground, perhaps anticipating an ambush if the zebra change direction.

Streaking through the sedge grass, the large female pursues the striped bedlam. But the chase soon appears impossible and, with a burst of speed, she turns her attention to buffalo. Michael's 600-millimetre lens whirrs and rattles at eight frames a second. A buffalo is an ambitious objective for a single lioness. The stampeding herd splashes through the swamp. White cattle egrets spill into the air squawking. Buffalo and lions disappear into the long grass and the ground thunders, reeds whipping in fury at the commotion beneath. Brooks guns the Land Rover, driving hell-for-

165

leather over the marshy ground, the vehicle bucking in the bumps. My handwriting squiggles on the notepad and the pen drips incontinently.

The noise ceases and the egrets land. On the other side of the swamp we come to a halt in front of 800 heaving buffalo. The ox-peckers have resumed their day already. Through the river reeds wanders the large lioness, a dejected expression on her face.

It's dark when we return to camp. Sandflies are stuck on my face and mosquitos have constructed small mounds on my arms. And back in my tent, typing up my largely illegible notes, tiny bugs attracted to the LCD screen fill the crevices of the keyboard. With every keystroke comes a macabre little crunch.

IT'S 5 AM and the sun is rising over the date palms like an angry mandarin. 'Watch out! Watch out!' Brooks squawks as we weave between thorny acacias. Past an indignant herd of 'buff' and a couple of elephants, skirting around the outside of 15 lions of the Matata pride and launching into Jiggajigga channel with a roar. We have an appointment. And rhinos don't like to be kept waiting.

Wilderness Safaris released five southern white rhinos, a species virtually wiped out last century, into Moremi National Park a year ago. They released five more last week, and today will introduce a further five in the hope of creating a sustainable breeding population.

Alison, a zoology grad from Florida State, perches atop the rhino enclosure and explains her obsession with the beasts. For the last couple of years she has been working in South Africa, Zimbabwe, Tanzania and Botswana, trying to rebuild the future for the animals. In Zimbabwe she hand-reared three young black rhinos in captivity. Poachers shot one as a warning and she had to flee the country, leaving behind the two others.

Her eyes fill with tears. 'My two girls are there and I don't know if they're alive.'

The whites marching around the wooden pen stand a better chance. All are between five and six years old, and Alison expects no territorial problems. 'In fact they will probably stick together for some time,' she suggests. Radio transmitters have been inserted into their horns to allow for tracking and recording of the animals' movements over coming years.

Michael and I bury cameras in a pile of dung outside the pen gate, discovering more magical properties of this material: it is firm, lightweight, malleable and makes perfect camouflage. We sit on the fence a couple of metres away with infrared remote controls in the hope of capturing the look on the faces of the newest wild rhinos in the world.

Alison slides back the gate. The rhinos peer nervously out of the gate then retreat back into the pen. The world must look a little too big. A minute later they ease from the compound, shuffling in the sand, and nose around the dung hill. Michael's camera clatters through the frames.

From my precarious perch I can see just how massive these creatures are, despite being sub-adult. The top of the shoulder is as high as a man and each weighs as much as a car. The bodies are muscle-bound, barrel-shaped masses, and tiny eyes puncture the skull low on the weighty head.

It's hard to imagine that these tremendous animals were hunted to the brink of extinction to satisfy a thirst for a superstitious sun-downer. It

white
rhino .

was believed in Arab high society that a drink made from the powder of a rhino horn was a powerful, if disgusting, aphrodisiac. They might as well have puréed their own fingernails.

The rhinos huddle in a group, their rumps pressed together. Nearby are several vehicles of European honeymooners wearing Versace jeans and architect glasses. The rhinos suddenly recall their rhino-ness and trot over to the cars, each a small enclosure of high-income *Homo sapiens*. She fiddles with her Gucci sunglasses, he adjusts his cravat. The rhinos watch in fascination for a while, regroup, and trot happily into the sun-drenched veld. Alison captures the moment: 'They're going off to be rhinos,' she shimmers, her face set with a smile of fulfilment.

IT'S A SHORT FLIGHT and the altimeter barely clicks over 150 feet. Tall acacias swoop under the wings and a huge plain of sedge is replaced by acres of permanent water. The Namibian government has run a pipeline north from the capital of Windhoek into the Okavango River in order to siphon off 5 per cent of the total flow for its parched city. Further downstream in Botswana that 5 per cent loss means a much greater reduction in flooded area. Angola is also investigating plans to dam the river for hydroelectric projects and an increase in agriculture will inevitably mean fertiliser run-off that could further threaten the future of the delta. Small changes have severe consequences.

The tyres *choop-choop* onto the Vumbra strip. The camp is small, immaculately appointed, and set within 65,000 hectares of wilderness with a reputation for big cats. A staff member introduces himself as Clinton, though colleagues appear to use a variety of permutations, the most popular of which seems to be 'Cliffy'. He's been a professional guide for more than ten years. Point to it, he can name it, and recite its taxonomy and a handful of little-known facts to boot. He is also the trainer for all the guides working in Wilderness Safaris' 37 camps.

Active page 168
Out-take: track the world's fastest animal with Cliffy.

'The delta's shrunk a lot in the decade I've been working here,' he tells me. 'It was about 18,000 square kilometres, now it's

Zebra employ patterns that dazzles any predator with lines and movement.

closer to 12,000.' Suddenly that sounds very small.

Vumbra had some early rains and the pans have turned a rich green, like a manicured golf course. And the best-dressed golfers are inspecting the fairway. Burchell's zebra are implausible-looking horses with a vivid full-body fingerprint, though the stylish lines look a darn sight better on the real thing than on cheap suede car-seat covers. A stallion chases a female in oestrus, biting at her rump for attention. She clamps her tail down hard and offers a solid discouraging kick. A typical kinship group would include a stallion and five or six of his favourite mares who submissively trot in order of rank.

In the 1970s the Botswanan government put up a veterinary cordon across the country. The plan was to control buffalo migration in the hope of protecting domestic cattle from the foot and mouth disease prevalent in buffalo. The move was intended to protect the agricultural industry and qualify the nation for funding from the World Bank after independence. No environmental impact report was compiled. The buffalo fences severed the migratory routes of many species between the Mobabe

Depression and the Savuti Channel. Most affected were herds of buffalo and zebra that could no longer reach traditional food and water sources. Since the fences were erected, zebra populations have been decimated – once 47,000 zebra made the migration, now the figure is closer to 6000. Buffalo numbers have been reduced by 50 per cent in Botswana.

Dark clouds, pregnant with rain, huddle over the delta. Shafts of light strike out from the belly of a silver cumulus. Thunder clouds roll thick on the horizon. An entire ecosystem holds its breath for rain. The feathery tops of three-awn grass glow. White-rumped babblers chatter.

A leopard strides across the thick green mat of sedge grass, the rosette patterns of its hooker-chic coat rolling as it moves towards the flood plain. Its white tail bobs with elegance. We stay about 100 metres away. Michael cautiously dismounts from the vehicle and the big cat stops immediately. It watches as Michael lies down on the ground with the 1200-millimetre lens. Cliffy positions the Landy to one side and ahead, so he can drive in front of Michael should the leopard exhibit more than healthy curiosity. It slowly turns its body to face the camera and drops to a crouch, pale eyes boring down the lens. Michael lies motionless but for his index finger, which pumps at the shutter frantically. In the 4WD we hold our breath.

Silently, inquisitively, the leopard rises a little, legs bent, head low, tail dragging. We are being stalked by a super-predator. The sensation is quite different to watching it stalk something else. Those eyes could cut glass. Just 40 metres from the car Michael makes a judgement call and leaps back in, unwilling to push his luck with a cat that could cover that distance in three seconds flat. We will have another opportunity to photograph the big cats of the Okavango.

THE RADIATOR HISSES like a scalded snake. Graham, the Wilderness Safaris guide from Duba Plains, is filling small bottles of water from the crocodile-infested swamp. It's midday, the temperature is over 40°C. There is a herd of water buffalo just ahead and a pride of hungry lions hunting within 100 metres. This must rate high on the list of Inappropriate Places to Overheat.

We drive on carefully, the Land Rover sinking deep into the marsh, four wheels in full diff-lock pulling hard. The buffalo are 500 metres ahead, wallowing in the sedge grass towards the north of the flooded plain. To follow them and their feline stalkers we will need to cross from Mokolwane Island to Old Mekore Station. The route corresponds with an inauspicious blank spot on the trail map: usually it's impassable. And it has no name.

The first serious obstacle is a large deep channel. Graham drives along the bank, eyes scanning for a possible crossing point. 'The water's too permanent here,' he decides. Permanent water is deep water. If it's too deep the car will be flooded, too muddy we'll get stuck, and if the opposite bank is too steep we'll never get out. What with the crocs, lions and buffalo it's a bit of a task.

Twenty minutes later we still haven't found a ford, and choose instead to see where the lions cross. Graham parks the Landy where we can see them waiting under an umbrella thorn acacia. We eat sandwiches, the radiator whistling merrily.

The Tsaro pride lions amble from the shade and walk past 2 metres from the driver's door. At least where the driver's door should be – it appears to have been misplaced or destroyed. Two lionesses stand on the bank for some time, evaluating the channel, and finally select a wide section with a sandy entrance. One by one they wade in, the water reaching their jaws. The obviously displeased young male holds its tail high.

Michael and Graham stand on the bank, hands on hips, in pointing, chin-rubbing appraisal. A combination approach is chosen: enter the channel where the lions did, but cross diagonally upstream to meet the bank where it is not so steep.

'Ready?' asks Graham.

It's a completely redundant question. Michael and I nod and the engine roars, a great bow wave peeling off the bull bars as we enter. We rock from side to side like a small ship in a giant swell, plumes of muddy water erupting from the wheel arches. The water sloshes around Graham's feet, a foot over the pedals. The right front wheel rides up on the opposite bank, screaming as it spins, flinging clods of river mud into the air. The vehicle slides sideways towards the river and Graham turns slightly pale. The tyres find traction again and we ride up the bank. He smirks with relief. 'I was wondering how I was going to explain that to the maintenance guy.'

We circle around the back of an island to find the sub-adult male has broken his cover and is trotting behind a group of stampeding buffalo. The lionesses look on indignantly. The buffalo assemble again in deep grass, mooing with delight. The lions wait in full view.

Graham ploughs the Landy into reeds so high we have to stand on the seats to see over the top. The radiator hisses. The tyres sink in the marsh. He lights a cigarette and drags hard, evaluating our predicament. There are hunting lions to our right, a herd of terrified buffalo ahead, crocs in the water, a deep channel to cross and the Landy has run out of coolant. 'I reckon when they go, we just go for it too.' All nod.

Dragonflies spin in circles. Graham is wet to his waist and covered with mud, engine grease and lashings of sunscreen, carefully pouring dirty water through an improvised filter. Flies torment me, orbiting my head and crashing into my ears. It's astounding how much frustration such a tiny insect can cause. We peer through binoculars, trying to judge the depth of water by the muddy waterline on the side of the lions.

Graham is cautious not to interfere with the animals and gauges their behaviour carefully. He waits until they have crossed. The bull bars of the Land Rover once again dip deep into the muddy swamp, wheels thrashing at the substrate for grip, and Graham pats the bonnet of the thirsty beast as we ride up the opposite bank.

Immediately we are surrounded by a massive black tide of mooing, grunting, chewing lion-feed. Buffalo have horns like handlebars, and small brown birds with brilliant yellow-and-red beaks chase parasites over their heaving bodies. Michael attempts a count. 'I would guess around 1500.' Sometimes it's easier to count the horns and divide by two.

Every surface of the Land Rover is roasting hot from the sun so I barely know where to rest my arms. My notebook is doubling as a sunshade and bug-whacking device.

The lions continue to advance. A group of five buffalo is some distance behind the main herd. It's a ready target and we race to position ourselves. The group is wandering towards a lioness, low in the long three-awn

Elongated hooves and powerful back legs help red lechwe bound through marshes.

grass. She waits. A large bull with thick horns and a line of ox-peckers riding his rump leads the way. Just 40 metres from the waiting predator he stops dead, raising his snout to the wind. With a start the bull turns on his heels and gallops back the way he came, the group in chaotic tow. Her cover exposed, the lioness dashes after them. She runs with a long bounding gait, head bobbing, muscles rippling. A wake of dust and flying grass follows the buffalo, which maintain a lead of 20 metres.

Graham primes us with a 'Hold on!' and we join the chase. The engine screams as he runs through the gears, rattling over the uneven plain. Grass and moths are dispatched from the bull bars and the front seat is showered with debris.

With a sudden burst the lioness catches up to the tiring buffalo and dances among them, selecting her prey. After a couple of quick diversions she leaps on to the back of a younger cow, her claws digging into the thick hide. The cow twists desperately and the lion tumbles to earth, immediately pouncing again with a stronger grip. The buffalo spins in tight circles with the lioness swinging full-length from him before coming unstuck and flying in a long trajectory in front of the large male. He lowers his horns to strike, and the lioness scampers for the cover of the trees. Buffalo 1, Lions 0.

We peer through binoculars and lenses in stunned silence. The engine is still running. From behind the vehicle the sub-adult male lion approaches. He's a little late to render assistance but right on time to spring a fresh attack. He advances at a trot. The buffalo resume their escape, rumbling around behind a thickly wooded island.

Graham selects a thin patch of wild date palms and slips through to appear on the other side at the same time as the lions. The two other cats are trying to outflank the herd to the north in a fatal game of move and counter. The young male makes another dash but after a chase of some 400 metres he gives up. The buffalo have entered the territory of a different pride. They are safe for another day.

Sand, dust and grass are stuck to sunscreen and sweat in a thick paste. The sun beats down mercilessly. Occupying the only shade for miles, the lions are lying under the broad branches of a sausage tree on a lonely island. Graham eases the Land Rover closer to the panting pride and one of the females moves aside, allowing us a spot out of the sun.

The relief is palpable. Graham looks above us to the heavy seeds of the sausage tree swinging in the breeze. 'This is not a good place to sit,' he says, somehow forgetting that four frustrated super-predators are lounging within metres of the vehicle. I can't help thinking the possibility of being topped by a falling fruit compares favourably to the alternative.

We eat sandwiches. I slouch back in the front seat with my feet kicked up on the bonnet. Graham does the same, navigating his legs around the steering wheel in an awkward fashion, and Michael dozes, using his camera equipment as a $30,000 pillow.

The lioness lies with her head between her paws. She is so close I can see my reflection in her yellow eyes, yet neither of us is particularly concerned by the presence of the other. There is a sense of community with the big cats: we share the shade of this tree and, in a larger sense, the custody of wild places like this. Once tourists brought rifles, now they pack cameras and an understanding of the environment. In Botswana's flooded Okavango the wilderness remains intact, if not unscathed.

WILD GUIDE

There are many safari companies in Maun catering for the full range of travellers – luxury accommodations and walking safaris, scenic flights and long 4x4 trips. Flights into the delta are usually organised by the camp of your choice and other organisations leave in *mekoro* canoes and stay in tents. One of the largest operators in the delta is Wilderness Safaris. The newest information is to be found simply by asking the pilots and guides lined up along the nearest Maun bar in the afternoon.

GETTING THERE

There are flights from most major cities to Johannesburg, from where you can fly daily to Maun on Air Botswana. Or you can drive. It's 1450 kilometres from Johannesburg to Maun. I know because I drove it once. It took just under 14 hours, including a two-hour snooze at 3 am just south of Francistown. The roads were occupied with an alarming concentration of donkeys, antelopes and the occasional black mamba snake choosing to loiter on the asphalt in the early hours of the morning to warm up.

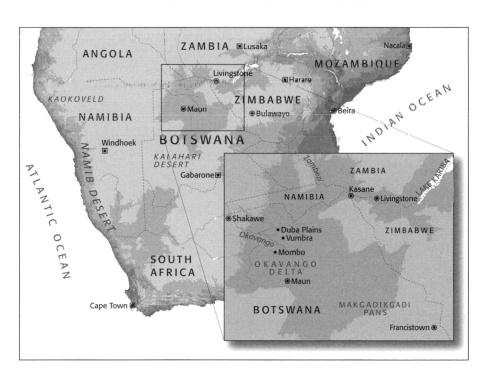

CONTACT

Wilderness Safaris
Johannesburg
South Africa
Tel: +27-11-807 1800
Fax: +27-11-807 2110

FURTHER READING

Richard D. Estes, *The Safari Companion*,
    Chelsea Green, 1999
Kenneth Newman, *Newman's Birds of
    Southern Africa*, New Holland
    Publishers, 2002

Ian McCallum, *Wild Gifts*, Russel
    Friedman Books, 1999
John Reader, *Africa – A Biography of the
    Continent*, Penguin, 1998

WEBSITES

National Geographic Cyber-Safari
    www.nationalgeographic.com/
    okavango/
Endangered Wildlife Trust
    www.ewt.org.za
Wilderness Safaris
    www.wilderness-safaris.com

Following pages *p. 177* A male hippo asserts his dominance. *p. 178* Ox-peckers pick ectoparasites from the back of a juvenile giraffe. *p. 179 (top)* A lioness, exhausted from the hunt, slumps in the sand beneath a sausage tree. *p. 179 (bottom)* Baboons use tools to feed and have even learnt how to open the window of a Cessna 206, much to the frustration of delta pilots.

agulhas to
benguela
COASTAL AFRICA

I'M SITTING on a red vinyl seat in a small room on a navy gunship surrounded by M16s and Tanzanian seamen. I am trying to convince them that in some countries you are only allowed one wife, but they seem to think it's a joke. 'Then how many children are you allowed?' queries the man with stars on his dirty lapels. Oh, as many as you like. 'That's strange.' And in this moment, in the sweaty bilge of the warship, it sounds unusual to me as well.

It's election time in Tanzania. The government was accused of rigging the election three years ago, and it is expected by many that the same will happen again. We escaped from Zanzibar at four this morning to

Left The population of the green and hilly island of Pemba has been infused with peoples from mainland Africa, the Middle East, and the Indian subcontinent.

A dhow carries cargo from Zanzibar's notorious Stone Town to Tanzania's old capital of Bagamoyo. In its heyday Zanzibar (in background) was one of East Africa's most prominent slave-trading markets.

flee escalating political unrest. Locals were apprehensive, everyone was on edge, so we steamed north to the atoll of Pemba.

After anchoring Michael noticed a gunship manoeuvring outside the channel. *Starship* has been mistaken for a military vessel before on account of its grey hull and the electronic rig on the mast, so we decided to take action before they turned their gun turret in our direction. A small party jumped in the tender and headed through the channel. We were waved alongside the frigate, smothered in a dense fog of fumes that made us cough uncontrollably and our eyes stream. The side deck of the vessel was lined with the entire crew of 30 men, many armed with automatic weapons; the rest appeared to be able to kill with their bare hands.

We had not checked in to Pemba because the port-control officials had all gone to vote. Evidently we should have contacted the Tanzanian navy instead. Ship's documents, crew lists and other paperwork were required to satisfy the captain. It was all back on *Starship*, and we were asked to take three very well-armed officers with us to retrieve it. And naturally they required that two of us be put under temporary arrest on the gunship.

So here I am, with Lasse the Swedish chef, held hostage on red vinyl seats, turning the conversation towards their task of patrolling the Tanzanian coast and trivia of monogamous society. They are nice guys, and after half an hour of hilarity we are allowed to reboard our tender.

An officer leans over the stanchion and apologises in my direction. 'I'm sorry, we don't usually arrest people,'

'No worries,' I reply with a genuine smile. I've never been arrested before.

FROM PEMBA we head west to Tanga where people greet us 'Salama sana' and Lasse breaks his toe on the boat ramp. Then south to Bagamoyo where once they shipped copra, ivory, salt and slaves to Zanzibar's market in sailing dhows. Then south again to Dar es Salaam, the fastest expanding city in Africa. The name means 'haven of peace' but I get mugged walking through a crowded market and have to fight to retrieve my wallet and my dignity. We pass the island of Chapyani where there is a cemetery for sailors and a headstone that reads simply 'Fell from aloft, age 15'. And the gyro-compass that steers the ship dies on my watch at 3 am, leaving us spinning circles in the Indian Ocean.

South south south, into the treacherous Mozambique Channel to the volcanic Comoros where a Muslim sultan rented the island to the French for 5000 francs a year in exchange for protection. South. South and east to Madagascar and a delightful port with an ugly name. Renault 4s putter through the streets of Hell-Ville where bougainvillea hangs from balconies and lemurs hang from trees. I see big green boa snakes and chameleons. Chameleons that change from lime green to jet black in the blink of an eye and roll out a 30-centimetre tongue in four-tenths of a second. And hot nights and rain storms with lightning that crackles to ground in five-pronged forks.

South to Nosy Mitsio where they bury their dead in canoes and where, at the beginning of the twentieth century, a warship of Russian sailors took leave of duty to live out their days in the tropics. South and south and west, zagging the zig, across the Mozambique Channel again to Joao da Nova, a tiny atoll occupied by terns, frangipanis and 15 French legionnaires. Enough stories to fill a hundred books.

And on through the South Indian Gyre, dodging a low-pressure system to Richards Bay where we refuel, provision, take on water and head south again. South down the Shipwreck Coast to East London, to Port Elizabeth and on through the seas haunted by the ghastly ghostly *Flying Dutchman*. Further south than *Starship* has been for a year. And around the cape where the Agulhas current meets the Benguela, past the Mail Tree where eastbound ships once left post for vessels returning to Europe. And west past Hermanus with a sign on shore that reads 'Please do not feed the whales' and around Cape Point where Captain Charles pours a shot of rum into the Atlantic to appease Neptune. Another day, another ocean, another city: Cape Town for Christmas.

Another year and another adventure awaits. South again, retracing our course around the Cape of Good Hope and into the dark waters of the Agulhas Bank.

BLOOD DRIPS from the tips of his fingers into the black Atlantic that swirls around South Africa's southern tip like a great wrinkled carpet. 'They will come,' he says with a wan smile on his face. He lights a cigarette carefully between bloody fingers and draws hard, 'Come on,' he coaxes again in a whisper, and lowers a ragged bouquet of barracuda into the water.

Michael Rutzen is a young commercial fisherman turned shark wrangler. Beneath the blood and scraps of bait a 20-centimetre-long scar runs the length of his forearm. He displays it like a trophy of war. 'There was a white shark a few weeks back that was a bit quicker than me,' he laughs, and drags on his cigarette again. 'Cut right through the artery and muscle too.'

He stuffs more shark liver into a mesh bag and hangs it over the stern of *Starship*. An oily slick begins to develop on the surface. 'A great white can detect a drop of liver oil from 500 metres,' Rutzen explains. 'They will come.' He adds a punctured plastic bottle of fish oil from the aft platform and the slick gathers weight.

All eyes are on the dark water, willing those small aberrations of contrast to take on more sharky forms. The sun rose just an hour ago and the low light catches the sea, sparkling in my eyes.

Almost immediately Lisa calls out a chilling exclamation from the foredeck: 'Shark!' Cameras are in hand, video rolls. A menacing shadow scribes a long radius from the bow of *Starship* to a position 20 metres off the stern, and then disappears.

The atmosphere is tense. I whisper and fidget, searching the waves in confusion. Suddenly a fin pierces the surface, approaching the boat obliquely. Michael kneels in a puddle of fish guts on the aft platform just metres from the water. His right hand holds an orange rope attached to the bloody mess of barracuda in the water. His left hand reaches out towards the oncoming shark as if to shake the hand of an old acquaintance. The fin rises. 'Don't move now,' he warns, leaning perilously over the stern, reaching long towards the predator, staring it down, counting off the metres in his mind. His left hand extends almost to touch and his right deftly lifts the bait from the water. Without altering its pace the shark feathers its broad pectoral fins, descends beneath the stern and disappears.

Nothing remains but heartbeats, and the faintest swirl in the water. I can't believe something so big could glide by so silently. The entire crew exhales as one and continues to scan the waves. Seconds pass. Frustrating minutes. The tension doesn't depart with the shark but lingers, reluctantly waning as the minutes click by. In a moment of resignation I switch the camera to standby.

Hours pass.

The wind has risen to 20 knots and swung to the south-east, a healthy current is running, the water temperature is only 13°C and underwater visibility has reduced to 3 metres. Andre Hartman is taciturn. Like a guru he passes judgement through his smoky beard: 'Not good.'

Andre has probably seen more great white sharks than anyone. He has looked into the eyes of these most feared predators and reached out to touch them a hundred times over. Andre may well know more about their behaviour than the scientists studying them, but then they don't know much – there are few definitive studies on great white sharks because they are so rare and so difficult to monitor. We do not know how long they live or where they mate and when. All we know for sure is that they are here in more abundance than anywhere, patrolling the southern tip of Africa.

The warm Agulhas current sweeps down the east coast and combines with the cold Benguela flowing up the west. In three large bays between the Cape of Good Hope and Danger Point a zone of shallow temperate water and a series of fur seal colonies create a small slice of heaven for a great white shark – and a haven for eco-tourism. A lucrative industry rides on the wave of shark paranoia conjured up in the mid 1970s by the book, then the film, *Jaws*. Novelist Peter Benchley struck a chord with his

Andre Hartman (foreground) began Gansbaai's shark tourism business when he discovered the great white's tonic response to a touch on the nose.

audience: 'People have always been terrified of sharks, of deep water, and of the unknown,' he wrote, 'and this story touched all those nerves.' Yet now, with the benefit of hindsight (and a few bucks in the bank) he concedes, 'I have become convinced too, that considering the knowledge accumulated in the past 25 years, I couldn't possibly write *Jaws* today, not in good conscience anyway.'

So why the about-face? A quarter century ago we thought that great white sharks ate people by choice and went into a feeding frenzy on scenting blood. We thought that they attacked boats. We thought they were malicious. Now we know that almost every attack on humans is accidental and three-quarters of all victims survive. Worldwide, only 69 fatal attacks by great white sharks have been recorded since 1876. A person is 3000 times more likely to be injured while installing a toilet than being attacked by any sort of shark anywhere...but then those plastic seats can really sneak up on a guy.

Sharks killed three humans in 2002. In the same year humans killed around 100 million sharks.

The most feared of all marine predators may in fact be in danger itself. Human exploitation of natural resources has touched every land-mass on earth, threatening or destroying species from the wettest rainforest to the driest desert. And in the last half century our reach has extended to include the open ocean. The world export of shark fins has risen from US$13 million in 1976 to over US$1 billion today. Once sharks were caught mostly by accident, but since the 1980s they have been targeted to feed an expanding international market. In a grotesque operation, sharks are dragged aboard a fishing vessel, where they have their dorsal and pectoral fins cut off. While they are still alive they are discarded back into the sea to die of starvation or be eaten by their own kind.

As an apex-predator with very few natural enemies, the great white grows slowly up to a maximum length of 7 metres, matures late, lives long and needs to produce only a few young. These characteristics have serious implications as fishing pressure increases. Scientists monitoring populations in the north-west Atlantic have recorded a 79 per cent decline in white sharks in the 15 years since 1986. In some areas no white sharks have been caught at all since the early 1990s. In an effort to counter this trend, South Africa protected the great white shark and other countries, including Australia, the Maldives, Namibia and parts of the United States, have since followed suit.

Our great white fails to return to the bait today and *Starship* heads back to Gansbaai.

WE COME AGAIN the next day, and the next, but it's as if the sharks don't exist at all.

On day four we wait, cameras within arm's reach, an air of gradually declining anticipation. *Starship* rolls from gunwale to gunwale in the ocean swell, objects clatter in the shelves and everyone feels a couple of shades south of their best. Lasse loads *Jaws* into the DVD player and we watch as a giant robot shark scares the wits out of pretty girls. The irony is difficult to escape, as is the uncanny likeness between Andre Hartman and the film's rogue shark fisherman Quint: 'I'll catch this bird for ya, but it ain't gonna be easy. Bad fish!'

Outside, beyond Hollywood's drama, we take turns to monitor the bait, searching the shadows for signs of life, peering through wave crests for a glimpse of the movie monster, for the fear that furnishes our legends.

A couple of days ago the shark boys thought it would be hilarious to give us a gift. They presented *Starship* with a toy great white shark that sings the Sinatra classic 'Mack the Knife'. Now every time a crew member passes rubber Frank they push the button and he launches into the opening bars: 'Oh the shark has pretty teeth, dear, and he shows them pearly white…' After three days the tune provokes streams of abuse and a hail of well-pitched objects aimed at the person daring enough to press the button.

By the end of the day the wind has increased. It's too rough to hoist the tender back onto deck and too windy to tow it. Some poor sod will have to drive it back to port. The poor sod in question is me. I don every piece of wet weather gear I own, toss a lifejacket over the top and lash myself to the ignition in the hope that if I get washed overboard by a big one the boat will stop.

It's only 8 metres deep in Walker Bay and the ocean swell stands up stiff and steep, with whitewater exploding on the crests. Even the 23-metre *Starship* pounds through this sea, and aboard the very much smaller tender, I regularly take to the air, launching off curlers with the propellers screaming for salt water. I feel like a *Baywatch* stunt-double – except I'm missing the Raybans and perfect curls of a California man-perm.

Other than a few big hits and half a dozen stomach-turning falls off the backs of breakers, both vessels make it home in one piece.

Day five is much like day four: lots of weather, no sharks. The perpetual rolling is getting to us. The sardine run ended a while ago and the great whites have probably followed it up the coast.

'Perhaps', 'Probably', 'Maybe', these are the words that begin every sentence on board *Starship* this week. We are living in purgatory, waiting on the caprice of a big fish, and it's making me antsy.

Starship ploughs through the breakers. (Video images: James Frankham)

As day six dawns calm we realise that a window of acceptable weather is opening, and the opportunity to round the notorious Cape of Good Hope is ripe. Just time for one more day on the station. The clock is ticking.

Again Michael Rutzen cuts up fist-sized chunks of offal and lashes corpses of stale fish to the stern. Again the smelly super-highway looms behind *Starship*. And again we wait.

'Haai op die ass!' calls Andre in Afrikaans – shark on the bait! In an instant the crew are assembled on the aft deck shoving away five days' delirium to find our senses. A bullish-looking shark circles tightly, its robust body grey like the hull of a Tanzanian frigate. Cameras on, tape rolling. This time I hurdle the gunwale to join the cowboy on the platform with fish guts and the Atlantic sloshing around my knees. This time I'm going for a toothy close-up. The camera is loaded in an aluminium underwater housing and tethered back to the boat.

Five days ago the 3-metre shark approached with caution. It was reasoned behaviour. This time it's a different animal altogether. The shadow is deep and barely detectable. It approaches fast, sweeping up to the boat acutely.

'This is a difficult one,' says Michael. 'It's coming up fast...and the eyes, you can see it in the eyes.'

The upper jaw of a great white is advanced and protruded to allow its participation in the biting action. The potential for rapid destruction is unparalleled.

It makes a couple of approaches from the stern as if testing the location of the bait. I watch the approaching shadow with my arm in the foggy water up the elbow, guessing the framing and drawing back the camera as the beast squares up to the chum bag.

Not close enough.

Suddenly the shark attacks from the broadside and before Michael can pull out the bait it has it in its jaws. Eyes roll back in blind violence, five rows of massive serrated teeth grip the line, it thrashes to free the fish. The powerful tail pounds the surface. The jaw is thrust forward to display a terrifying array of daggers that crush the plastic oil bottle and tear at the barracuda. Michael reels back, the rope burning through his fingers. The noise. The power. The massive body bounces square off the face of my lens. Pure aggression. Finally the bait line shears and recoils back into Michael's chest with a crack.

The beast descends again. I expect I got close enough that time.

Michael's sentences are short and his voice holds a quiver of urgency just short of panic.

'Look out! Look out!' he shouts, leaping across the stern platform to reset the line. If there is no bait there is no focus for the shark and it could confuse anything with a food source, even the tender.

Michael's angry with himself. He broke his own rule; the shark should never take the bait. Slashing at the remains in the bait bucket, he frantically cuts up another section of foul fish, constantly checking over his shoulder like a nervous thief.

I am wet to my waist and my hands shake. Fear courses through my veins like caffeine. At one moment the shark was cruising with ghastly precision, and in the next it bombarded like a raging tank. I'm not sure how I feel about this shark wrangling. I'm impressed by the animal, but a little disturbed by the method of contact. This is by far the most aggressive interaction we have had with animals on the *Starship* voyage and though the animals come to us, I'm not convinced we haven't crossed some undescribed ethical boundary. Yet the sharks show no fear or obvious stress, and the behaviour we hope to see can be recorded no other way.

An hour later we're still kneeling on the platform. My legs hurt, where

I'm wet I'm cold, and the camera housing feels like it weighs a tonne. Journalist Jan Wiechmann is interviewing Michael: what would you have done if it had pulled you into the water? 'I wouldn't panic, I'm not his prey or his competition,' says Michael matter-of-factly. Would you try to swim out of its way? presses Jan 'Swim? No.' Why not? 'Because I can't swim,' admits the shark wrestler.

When Andre Hartman began working with great white sharks in this way he became the centre of worldwide intrigue. And controversy. 'Operators continually sensationalise encounters with these animals and foster an incorrect image of sharks,' says Chris Fallows, a local shark enthusiast. For nearly ten years he has been researching the great whites, photographing and identifying each individual and building up a database that gives clues to their movements and behaviour. He has spent weeks waiting with his finger on the shutter for a single photo of a white shark breaching. And when he succeeded it hit the front page of newspapers from Canada to New Zealand, accompanied, to his horror, by the sensationalist straplines he despises: 'Killer on the Loose' and 'Be Afraid, Be Very Afraid'.

Chris is concerned by the effects of shark tourism. 'Eco-tourism is a very positive way to show people just how fantastic sharks are, but they must be handled properly,' he says. 'They can be injured by hitting outboards, swallowing ropes or just disturbed from their natural hunting patterns.' But inside Gansbaai's flourishing tourist industry he is dismissed as a fanatic. Conservation worrywart or prophet, only time will tell.

A large dorsal slices through the oily surface and disappears like a descending periscope.

'Here's a player,' calls Michael.

My camera follows underwater, the Atlantic chill prickling my arm. The shark lunges suddenly at the bait but misses, the cowboy teasing it back out of reach of the thrusting jaws. It bites again, misses again and rises, head out of the water, following the practised hand. The jaws are exposed and Michael tenderly touches the underside of the snout with three fingers, and the shark lifts higher in reflex. Another touch and the 4-metre shark is standing vertically, suspended in a trance beneath

Michael's conjurer hand. It hangs motionless for seconds before tilting backwards to lie catatonic on its back, displaying the white belly that gave the species its name. The great tail swishes

Active page 193
'Starship Troopers Invade City' – read an article from the *Cape Argus*

gently. Half a dozen strokes and it regains its composure, rolling over and descending in a daze into the deep.

Michael Rutzen kneels on the aft platform, following the disappearing caudal fin with his gaze. Chris Fallows stands on the top deck, admiring without touching, and Andre Hartman puffs on a cigarette and nods. All wear an expression of recognition and fresh wonderment. The bold cowboy, the fanatical conservationist and the wizened wrangler are driven by the same desire to discover the secrets hidden behind the jaws of the great white shark. Why is this powerful animal intoxicated by the slightest touch? Is it an overload of sensory information or an interruption of it? The experts are confounded.

Driven by instinct the massive carnivore returns again and again, each time rising powerful from the water to hang beneath Michael's touch and slide back down again mesmerised. And every contact seems more familiar, calmer. The eighth time is the last. The mighty shark rolls over, its curiosity expended, and descends into the shadows without returning. The glassy water closes over the top in a delicate vortex.

Starship's engine rumbles, the calm water indicative of a storm front rising in the south. The narrow gates of the Cape of Good Hope are closing and we must start our passage north.

IT'S DARK as we round the cape, running with the Benguela current up the coast. The night is clear and moonless. A ruffled sheet of green water peels off the bow, alive with bioluminescence. The intensity is such that it lights the underside of the hull.

Leaning over the bow on my 2 am watch I reflect on the sharks, on the excitement and terror of last few days. It seems we are making some of the same mistakes in the sea as we have made on the land. It is the same lack of understanding that allowed indigenous cultures to destroy forests for short-term agricultural benefit and European colonials to introduce destructive species of plants and animals. Overfishing, low-frequency active sonar, pollutants and the indirect effects of land-based industry are destroying our oceans. And the depths are not an inexhaustible supply of regenerating providence, as we once thought.

I am joined by a pod of Heaviside's dolphins. They are found nowhere else on the planet and thrive in the fish-intensive ecosystem that the cold current inspires. Small and fast, they have beautiful markings, a silver saddle from the snout to the dorsal fin that runs down the flank, sweeping back as if coloured by the contour of the water. But tonight the markings are invisible. Instead the dolphins are luminous green, shimmering and dazzling, dancing like tiny torpedoes around the bow and surfing on our displacement wave.

It's an intimate light show for me, their only audience. I peer over the forward railing entranced. With barely a flick of a tail, hardly a movement of a fin, they duck and dive, feed and free ride, perfectly sonar-synchronised with their wing-partners. Vapour trails of excited phyto-plankton tear off their pectoral fins like an aerobatic show, up the African coast, on towards Namibia.

WILD GUIDE

The high season for shark watching at Gansbaai coincides with the South African winter – May to October – when stormy weather is just a fact of life. Conditions can prevent boats from going out to sea, but once they launch the chance of seeing sharks is virtually 100 per cent. The weather is better a month or two either side of the winter season, but shark sightings drop to about 70 per cent. You'd be lucky to see one during the summer, but it is still possible. If you are happy to bait the sharks and a bit of wrangling doesn't offend your environmentalist sensibilities then go out with Andre Hartman for a day. Or talk to Chris Fallows, who takes a different approach. You will get plenty of action but witness more natural behaviour. Using Chris's innovative observation techniques there is a reasonable chance of seeing a great white shark breaching. He runs 10-day shark safaris but can also cater for shorter tours.

GETTING THERE
Flights from major cities worldwide come to Cape Town's international airport.

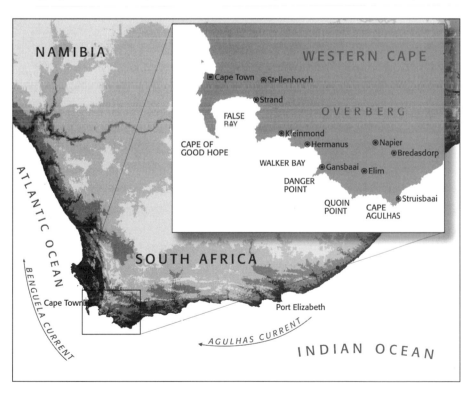

Gansbaai is 170 kilometres south-east of Cape Town and it takes two hours to reach it by road. If you have your own transport take the N2 out of Cape Town, then drive over Sir Lowry's Pass and Houhoek Pass. At Bot Rivier take the R43 to Hermanus, drive through Hermanus and past Stanford and continue on to Gansbaai. Between Gansbaai and Hermanus there are more than a hundred different places where you can stay.

CONTACTS
Andre Hartman
Email: kula@mweb.co.za

Chris Fallows
Tel: +27-82-364 2738
Email: sharky1@mweb.co.za

WEBSITES
Marine Dynamics
   www.dive.co.za
Apex Predators – Chris Fallows
Photography
   www.apexpredators.com
African Eco-Charters
   www.ultimate-animals.com
International Shark Attack File
   www.flmnh.ufl.edu/fish/Sharks/ISAF/
   ISAF.htm
Gansbaai website
   www.gansbaai.net

FURTHER READING
Peter Matthiessen, *Blue Meridian*,
   Penguin, 1997
Peter Benchley and David Doubilet,
   'Great White, Deep Trouble', *National
   Geographic*, April 2000

Following pages *p. 197* Michael Rutzen wrangles sharks for a living. 'It's about concentration,' he suggests. 'You have to know which way the shark is going to move next.' *pp. 198–9*. Rutzen reaches out to touch as the practised killer slides by. The author quivers on the end of the underwater video camera.

kaokoveld
NAMIBIA

CAMERON IS the quintessential pilot: young, dashing, crew-cut and whiskered, with mirrored sunglasses that slide under the earphones. He eases the Cessna into the Namibian air – reading the weather report as we climb. The altimeter passes 3000 feet and we level out, the bush veld rippling over small hills all the way to the horizon. The soil beneath us phases from green to pasty ochre, yellow sand to orange gravel, red lichen, dry grey flood channels and finally a monumental ridge of dark rock. Creased with time, this area is at least 80 million years old.

Rocky hills laced with green vegetation give way to the red sands of the world's oldest desert. The ancient Namib stretches out before us. Wind-

Left An oryx surveys Porros Plain at dawn. Many of the Namib's animals are active in the early morning, relying on moisture in the air as their only source of water.

contorted dunes squirm, striated by dry riverbeds, highways for a vast array of wildlife. A herd of the rare desert elephant meanders up the dry Huab River. A flock of ostriches scatters in confusion, unable to discern the direction of the aircraft. The Cessna drops low, descending into a valley to catch a glimpse of an oryx, a stunning painted antelope. Unfazed, it stares straight back, convinced that the screaming steel bird is no threat.

A blue edge is appearing between the sand and sky and anticipation grows. We are approaching one of the most notorious coastlines in the world. The plane thunders through thermals rising from the colossal dunes that mark Namibia's Skeleton Coast. Beneath us white water pounds relentlessly on the shore. Cameron steers onto a new course along

The European quest for the markets of the Orient was blocked by the World of Islam, and this sea route against the wind and the current, through dense sea fog, without shelter or provision for water, became quickly known as the Skeleton Coast.

the surf line and the aircraft becomes quiet, no longer battered by turbulent air.

Through the starboard window there is a desert wasteland. And through the port an endless expanse of ocean. Sea mist hangs in the air, obscuring the distant horizon and giving the impression that the beach must stretch northward forever. It feels like I have arrived at the very edge of the world.

A nondescript hulk is awash in the breakers. Wrecks like this one are dotted along the length of the coast, the remains of ships foundered on the treacherous rocks with little hope for the crew – even if they survived to reach land. Early navigators regarded this beach with fear, and a small measure of superstition because this is a land of no mercy, a hostile environment with little tolerance for the unprepared. Bodies were rarely recovered.

Cameron is a bloke who enjoys his job. He began flying in South Africa, worked in the Okavango Delta, and now confidently pulls on the ailerons, banking inland into a region marked on the map as 'Kaokoveld'.

'Welcome to nowhere,' he smirks.

Namibia is one of the most sparsely settled regions on earth, with a population density of less than two people per square kilometre. No less than 100,000 square kilometres have been dedicated to nature reserves ranging from arid to subtropical. A plume of dust marks our touchdown in one of the most famous of these reserves.

Our guide Shadreck blinks and grins enthusiastically in the bright daylight as we bundle into his Land Rover. He's got the confident persona of a football star, and a gag for every occasion. Michael makes a quick quip about his shaved head and Shadreck replies, 'This is my hairstyle, it's weatherproof.'

With the low-ratio gearbox whining in first gear we shimmy through the axle-deep sand with Shadreck telling us the lonely story of Namibia's most remote region. The Skeleton Coast is easily the driest area in Namibia, recording barely 6 millimetres of rain each year. And where conditions are extreme, a small number of species evolve to take advantage of tiny ecological niches.

Shadreck stops the vehicle, and we get out and tiptoe over the gravel, taking care not to leave any footprints because they will stay forever. Shadreck leads us to an outcrop of innocuous-looking rock where he points out a miniature lobed succulent called a lithop. It absorbs water vapour from fog; every 80 to 100 years it grows another lobe about the size and shape of a peanut. My mum's pansies last a season, but clinging to the edge of this magma outcrop is a three-lobed lithop, probably well over 200 years old. It's a miraculous achievement for a minute pink squishy thing.

The beauty of the desert flora is subtle, reflecting the environment but somehow at odds with it. And the balance is precarious. The introduction of one new species would alter the equilibrium and almost certainly result in the disappearance of another. Isolation has preserved the rugged beauty of the Skeleton Coast, and one must touch it lightly, if at all.

A wind known locally as the Soo-oop-wa sighs eerily as it rides over the crest of barchan dunes, carrying with it clouds of sand. Particles of silica sand caught in the evening light wink at me, as if they know something I don't.

As night falls we make our way back to camp, my ears ringing in the silence. Tomorrow we hope to make contact with the Himba, a remote group of indigenous Namibians who roam this region with their cattle. I fall asleep dreaming of nomads, deserts and mum's pathetic pansies.

THE AIR IS CRISP, the sand cold. The doors snap into the catches and we pull off to head into the heart of the Kaokoveld. At home I work late, rise late and enjoy long breakfasts. But in the field I revel in these early-morning departures. The day is new and full of expectation.

We follow the dry Khumib River 'upstream', bouncing along the undulating riverbed. This river flows just one year in ten during torrential downpours, yet ground water beneath the dusty surface supports the mopane tree vegetation usually found in environments with more rain. The road is rough and we ricochet around the interior of the Landy like popcorn. Penyus bounces around on the back seat. He's wearing a blue shirt, a flimsy moustache, and a gummy smile, and is blessed with the quiet nature of many rural Africans. He's with us today because he speaks the language of the Himba, one of the last pastoral peoples of southern Africa.

We are bound for a small settlement called Otjovaurwa, a Herero word meaning 'loneliness'. From this semi-permanent settlement a handful of Himba eke out an existence in a hostile environment and, through their isolation, retain one of the most intact indigenous cultures in the world.

We lurch onto a featureless plain of gravel broken only by a four-wheel-drive road. This is how I imagine the surface of Mars: orange sand, red granite rocks and miles of nothingness. The sun is rising and the sky is blood red, the hills taking on a citrus hue. The sky is enormous, still sparkling with stars. I can only grin stupidly.

A solitary oryx breaks the skyline, blackened in silhouette. It turns to face our small group, hunched behind cameras on the side of the road. It's a work of art – the white face is war-painted with brown stripes, its beige body features striking brown markings along the flank. And on top of its head is an incredible rig, horns well over a metre in length standing tall, proud and gently curved. Perfectly adapted to the harsh environment, the oryx condenses water from the morning air behind an array of capillaries on its snout. The water drips onto the back of the tongue to sustain life. This is not an animal struggling at the brink of subsistence but rather one whose adaptations have allowed it to thrive in harsh conditions.

We set off once more; there is a great distance to cover today. Ostriches run alongside the vehicle, not realising that a change of course would yield a more effective getaway – more speed than brains. Shadreck grips the wheel and swaps through the gears furiously. Bucking and diving, we traverse the tracks of those who have gone before us, pushing deeper and deeper into the heart of the desolate Kaokoveld, now many kilometres from the safety of radio contact.

The camera gear slides perilously from one side to another in rhythm with our bodies. And the further inland we travel the worse the ride gets. The tracks of other vehicles turn off the riverbed and we are left on a

The banks of the Khumib River are littered with reminders of the paucity of water.

course of our own, untravelled since last this river flowed. A solitary sign swings from a broken stake. It's the first we have seen, ominously indicating that we are leaving Skeleton Coast National Park. It has taken over an hour to cover 30 kilometres.

The sun peers over the hills and the red dissolves. Orange clouds skate high above us. Leaning forward over the wheel, Shadreck squints in the burgeoning daylight. 'The trees around here have learnt how to talk.'

'A-ha,' I reply, waiting for one of his gags. But this time he's not joking. Shadreck explains above the whining gearbox that mopane trees release tannin when grazing animals eat them. The tannin makes the leaves bitter. It's a clever adaptation, but more incredible still, trees share this information: The smell of the tannin is carried on the wind and the mopane trees downwind also release tannin as a precautionary measure. Not to be outdone by smart plants, giraffes have learnt to graze progressively in an upwind direction, catching each tree by surprise.

Shadreck wipes the dust from his neck and finishes the story with consolation for my numb posterior. 'We're getting close.'

Up ahead a herd of cows blocks the road. It makes an odd sight in the middle of the desert. They look healthy, well fed, well watered. And in a deep hole I can see the reason: the bobbing head of a Himba herdsman. He's wearing a khaki drill shirt with large breast pockets and brass-buttoned lapels. An orange *kikhoi* is wrapped tightly round his midriff and hitched up to his knees. A necklace made of shells circles his neck. And in the middle of a desert that receives no more than 2 millimetres of rain in any given year, he stands up to his knees in water.

The hole he has dug is deep enough to reach into the water table of the dry Khumib River. A cigarette bobs between his lips as he shovels bucket-loads of water into a rickety trough. The cows lap vigorously. The fancy shirt is a trophy of his profession; he is a game ranger administering this quarter of the northern Kaokoveld. A job is a rarity in this isolated corner, though he finds time to tend his cattle, which are still the symbol of true status to the Himba.

Penyus exchanges a few words of greeting, smiling and touching the man's arm as he speaks, in the way old friends share a joke. The man nods in appreciation at each one of us in turn. We nod back, and he points further northward, rolling off a few more indecipherable words. Penyus nods. And we nod. Then set off again in our roaring Land Rover, nodding our thanks.

A cluster of dome-shaped huts circles the top of a small hill beneath the mountains. A fierce wind is whipping dust clouds into eddies. We skirt around the side of the village before coming to rest some distance away. Penyus has already warned us of the most critical rule of the Himba: never pass between their fire and the enclosure where the goats are held. This would be the greatest cultural *faux pas* in Himba society, perhaps because these symbols embody survival and wealth.

A small group of people huddles beneath blankets around a steaming pot. Mangy dogs wait in avid attendance. To one side a group of women painted red from head to foot sits cross-legged, sharing a pipe and blowing the smoke skyward.

Sheepishly we climb out of the Land Rover, feeling somewhat conspicuous. Shadreck and Penyus greet the elders and we exchange soft handshakes with Kamaseetu, the patriarch, and sit down. There is a moment of nervousness for both parties. Unusual visitors, unfamiliar hosts. But soon enough an awkward dialogue begins. It starts with longwinded introductions about us, our journey, our desire to meet them and then of this tribe, its background, relationships and settlement. We're all relieved to get the formalities out of the way and on to more familiar territory – the weather. Everybody gets stuck in, nodding enthusiastically and comparing yesterday to today, last week to this week and this morning to predictions for the afternoon. It's always a winner. The weather is universally intriguing, particularly to people who are at its whim, like nomads…and boaties.

As the conversation wanders on to other things, a couple of the women take the opportunity for a re-coat. Himba women smear their bodies with a paste made of red ochre, butterfat and aromatic herbs. In part it serves as protection from sun and wind, though the cosmetic value is probably more significant – it makes their skin appear incredibly smooth. They rub it on vigorously like a thick lacquer, and I suspect the act of applying the stuff would stimulate circulation and noticeably warm the body. There is a striking resemblance between the colour of their painted skin and that of the cattle. Perhaps both are symbols of prosperity for the group: women and stock, fertility and fortune.

The women's hair is twisted into dreadlocks with an ochre paste and accessorised with pieces of copper and buttons from military uniforms. Despite the cold wind, their tops are completely bare, with only simple leather garments draped around the waist. They wear bands around their wrists and ankles and metal adorns their hair and fingers. Animal skins are tucked in to heavy leather belts and a headband of copper latticework is propped up among the dreadlocks. Hanging below twisted copper neck rings is a large white conch shell, a symbol of marital status. It doesn't seem unusual until you realise that the conch is only found on the tropical east coast of Africa. The Himba are a trading people, part of a circuit that begins in Mozambique and extends clear across the continent to

Angola and down the coast to Namibia. By the time goods reach the Himba they have accumulated immense value. It is rare to find any woman over 20 years old not wearing this ornamentation, indicating the wealth of the Himba, once among the richest Bantu-speaking pastoralists in Africa.

The children wear beaded necklaces and their hair is tied up in complex braids, layered and pushed forward over the brow. They are naked but for a string of beads around their waists.

Kamaseetu draws on a loosely constructed cigarette. His eyes are old and wizened, his brow furrowed like the folding valleys of the Khumib itself. His beard is white. He seems at one with the land and nonplussed by his visitors. While the women and children are quick to interact,

kamaseetu's cloak.

Kamaseetu is more reticent. Quiet, calculating, suspicious, almost regretting our presence as an intrusion in an otherwise perfectly normal afternoon. I do my best to bridge the distance between our cultures and smile over the simmering pot. But I don't know if my efforts are unnoticed or ignored.

Perhaps Kamaseetu's silence is a reflection of a grudge against white people, well established over years of guerilla warfare during Namibia's quest for independence and the near-genocide that took place at the turn of the century under the German colonial power.

Maybe it's a show of opposition to national development. The Namibian government has proposed a hydroelectric project on the Kunene River just to the north that will deliver enough electricity in one day to power the capital of Windhoek for a year. Cheap energy, it is hoped, will stimulate foreign investment in the developing country. But the key to national development undermines the traditional economy of 9000 indigenous people that live in the region – 380 square kilometres of grazing land would be lost, pushing Himba that frequent the valley to the surrounding area, which will become overgrazed in a very short time. Overgrazing leads to erosion and desertification, a blight that directly affects 100 million people.

Kamaseetu must be sick of interference.

But we persist and, it seems, finally win his tolerance if not his acceptance. Shooting on digital cameras means that we can share an image with our hosts. Perhaps for the first time they understand what the large black objects actually do. The women giggle at the results and insist on more pictures. Some run back to their tents and dress in ceremonial costume, others bring out rudimentary musical instruments and are thrilled when they hear themselves played back on the MiniDisc recorder. We establish a currency of trust, and through Penyus ask more questions about their settlement.

The women ask if we can take them to the ocean in our Land Rover. Many of them have never been to the coast and they seem at least as excited by the idea of riding in a vehicle as in getting to the beach itself. We negotiate to transport some firewood from the river instead, though

Himba women pass between them a small metal pipe stashed with the bark of a tree very similar to tobacco.

they seem a little disappointed by such a pragmatic response.

The children get stuck in to a steaming pot of *mil-pap*, a glue-like food made of pounded millet, common across all of Africa. It tastes of little and is difficult to swallow but fills hungry stomachs. The kids dive in with hands and sticks – though the adults don't eat in our presence out of respect, or possibly because there isn't enough to go around. The dogs watch on. Two young boys wander off into the hills with a herd of goats. Massive magma ridges dwarf the pair and their hoofed entourage.

211

A light cloud of dust rises from their feet and they shimmer in the late afternoon heat.

And I wonder if I could exist in this hostile environment, lonely and lost to the world.

Herding has been the focus of Himba life since the introduction of cattle to southern Africa 2000 years ago. The entire community moves regularly, depending on local availability of pasture and water for the herd. In the 1980s the worst drought in living memory cost the Himba some 130,000 head of cattle. The effect upon the tribes in northern Namibia was devastating and many were forced to seek jobs in urban centres. Within a decade many tribes were lost to the homogenising effects of western culture and corrupted by the ills of modern Africa. Though government testing indicates a 20 per cent HIV infection in Namibia, unofficial estimates indicate that as many as 50 per cent of Himba test positive.

A young girl loads a donkey with water and food to take to herdsmen in the field. Old Kamaseetu assists as she struggles to lift the heavy plastic jerry cans and hurdle onto the beast, bareback. Although no more than eight years old she heads out into the wilds of the desert alone, riding a brute of a donkey and herding another before her. Into the setting sun she zigzags, naked but for a layer of red paste and a string of beads.

As the sun retreats behind the hills, the Himba women run back to huts and don more shiny jewellery, symbols of wealth from another time. A group of five assembles and a small crowd of onlookers circles them, giggling expectantly.

Somewhat bemused we set up cameras with wide-angle lenses so that we are ready for anything. 'What's going on?' Michael asks. Penyus just scratches his head.

A whirlwind dances dusty between the huts and wind rumbles in the microphone. A nervous group of performers begins clapping in a huddle, melodic chants rising as they summon stage courage. The women sing low and soft for some time, until an explosion of energy takes us all by surprise. Screaming, one of the women leaps into the air, red dust flying. She stomps and flails, leather garments sail behind her. The four other performers clap loudly, yelling and goose-stepping until the soloist runs across the village, clouds of dust following her. I am wide-eyed, panning left and right to find my vanishing subject. Michael peers

Active page 213
Watch the ancient Otjiunda dance.
Download the video clip.

through his zoom lens with similar bewilderment.

This is the Otjiunda dance. A woman plays a predator within the stock enclosure and the others form an imaginary kraal and attempt to scare her out. Every aspect of the Himba way of life seems to reflect the struggle against a hostile environment. Again and again the dance is performed, each time more vigorously, with rising support from the onlookers. Grins break out, but it's not until Michael decides to simulate the dance, his arms beating like a windmill, that hilarity really soars. These moments of understanding between dissimilar cultures are rare. Ditching feelings of uneasiness that we may do the wrong thing, we all find ourselves screaming with laughter.

We share the warmth of the fire into the evening, the embers from their tobacco making tiny orange stars beneath the banner of white ones. It's cold and windy. The feeble warmth of the fire provides little comfort and I shiver inside my Gore-Tex.

While the Himba have been known to inhabit this area since the 1920s, their isolation has meant that only a little is understood of their culture. However, the inevitable westernisation is occurring at an astonishing rate and there is a mere handful of settlements still living according to the traditions of past generations.

Another woman arrives with water. In one hand is a traditional hide pouch, in the other a plastic jerry can. Adapting quickly and innovatively is precisely in line with the fundamental tenets of the Himba. A subsistence society will always seek out the most effective solution. Choosing plastic in preference to animal skin is an obvious innovation, as are shoes and T-shirts.

We leave after some time and head back to our own camp, bouncing around on the riverbed, the yellow glow of the headlights illuminating the way ahead. It's repetitive and mesmerising and we're all contemplative. One image is stuck in my mind: that small huddle of humanity we left sheltering by the warmth of a fire, on a hill, in the middle of a desert, on the outskirts of civilisation and survival. And the face of Kamaseetu, riddled with angst.

Filming today I had the distinct feeling that I was recording material for the archives. I'm a little sad but I draw some consolation from Himba folklore. They understand time as a river, and they stand on the bank looking downstream. The river flows past and they watch and learn and tell stories of what has been, in order to understand what will come. The hydroelectric project will probably go ahead and the ancient pastoral lands of the Kunene will be flooded; the people displaced. And the great deluge of development will swamp Kamaseetu's people as well, bringing the best and worst of modern society, just as it has penetrated every other corner of the globe. But the fundamental struggle has not changed greatly for Kamaseetu. The survival of his people depends, as it always has, on their ability to adapt.

WILD GUIDE

The most pristine region of the Skeleton Coast Park, Namibia, is strictly off-limits to visitors. An exception has been made by the Directorate of Environmental Affairs giving access to one operator only, Wilderness Safaris, which runs a camp on the Khumib River. The luxury tented camp is pricey but exceptional. For those unwilling or unable to fork out for the exclusive experience, overland 4x4 operators extensively explore the northern Kaokoveld region for a fraction of the cost – check out *GetAway* magazine's website for more information. Alternatively get a group together, hire a 4x4 with plenty of spare tyres, water and a GPS, and go bush for a bit.

GETTING THERE
Major airlines fly out of Cape Town, South Africa, to Windhoek, Namibia, on a daily basis.

CONTACT
Wilderness Safaris
Johannesburg
South Africa
Tel: +27-11-807 1800
Fax: +27-11-807 2110

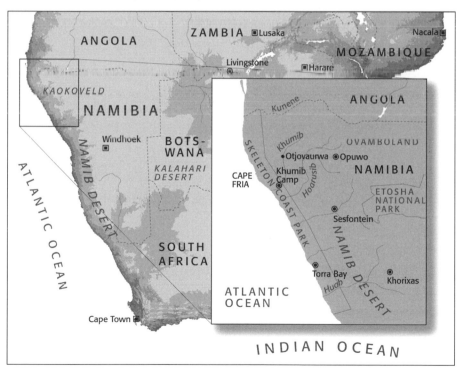

FURTHER READING

Margaret Jacobsohn et al, *Himba: Nomads of Namibia*, Struik, 1990

David P. Crandall, *The Place of Stunted Ironwood Trees: A Year in the Lives of the Cattle-Herding Himba of Namibia*, Continuum, 2000

David Campion and Sandra Shields, *Where Fire Speaks: A Visit With the Himba*, Arsenal Pulp Press, 2003

WEBSITES

Directorate of Environmental Affairs
www.dea.met.gov.na

Wilderness Safaris
www.wilderness-safaris.com

Geological Survey of Namibia
www.gsn.gov.na

Guide to Namibia
www.africa-insites.com/namibia

GetAway magazine
www.getawaytoafrica.com

Following pages *p. 217* A juvenile Cape fur seal saunters into the Atlantic. *pp. 218–9* Himba women take extraordinary pride in their adornments, which are fashioned primarily with leather, ochre and metal scraps. The white conch shell is most highly prized.

baboon island
THE GAMBIA

'JI CEFFYL BACH yn carlo ni'n dau, oho, ho,' Stella's mother used to sing to her, cradling her in her arms and patting her back in kindness. As an adult Stella used the same comforting gesture with another troubled girl, perhaps even singing the Welsh lullaby in her mind. She nurtured the four-year-old Nini, and though she wasn't Nini's biological mother she was a distant cousin. Nini was a chimpanzee. The very special relationship between Stella and Nini sowed the seed for a remarkable conservation project that would eventually restore hope for an endangered species and absorb a lifetime of devoted motherhood.

*

Left River Gambia National Park consists of five islands, the largest of which is Baboon Island.

AS WE POWER up the Gambia in *Starship* the river closes in to a channel a few hundred metres wide, the distance shrouded in fog. Stella Marsden's camp is 240 kilometres up-river, deep in the wild heart of Africa's smallest country. The Republic of The Gambia follows the course of the river for 350 kilometres, and is barely 50 kilometres at its widest. British colonials defined the breadth of the nation as the distance a cannonball could be shot from a frigate in the river, plus or minus a few kilometres. Bless those Brits.

On the electronic chart by which we steer the ship, the Gambia River ends abruptly in a brown line, as if it crashes into a wall of land. This is no place for a ship, but we plough on, using old paper charts as a guide. All eyes are fixed on the sonar's sweeping electric eye, scanning underwater for obstructions or patches of shallow in the ever-shifting riverbed. On each side are the rusting hulks of vessels that got it wrong, came too close, went too far. Now they are little more than perches for pelicans and spoonbills. At some points the river runs deep and fast, with more than 6 metres below our keel, but where it is wide it is also slow and shallow, *Starship*'s wake turning distinctly brown as she stirs up the substrate. 'Are you beginning your farming career?' jokes Lasse. But Captain Martin's eyes are on the sonar. Michael shuffles a parallel rule over the chart, observing the multitude of variations and notes on revised positions of islands and sand banks. He plots a course for the next few nautical miles and calls the coordinates out to Martin, who plugs them into the computer. The electronic system is convinced we are making ten knots over dry ground.

James Island appears on the chart. At last, after travelling half way around the world, I finally get to see an island bearing my name. It could be a perfect coral atoll with white beaches and palm trees, or a majestic spire of rock teeming with birdlife. But no such luck. James Island is probably the ugliest, most forlorn crop of soil to ever break the surface of the water. It's no more than a hundred metres across and covered with dead or dying trees. A fort lies in ruins at the centre. The island has been occupied by nearly every colonising power since 1651 and was notorious as a trading post for bootlegged gold, silver, ivory and finally slaves. The

The beautiful James Island offers secluded accommodations for those inclined to a more rustic ambience. Bring your own roof; whippings in the courtyard at midday.

most famous slave of all time, Kunta Kinte of the *Roots* saga, suffered beatings on this very spot. What a tribute.

The river is a rich caramel-brown and glassy calm. The banks are thinly covered with bush and every 500 metres or so there is a quiet settlement of thatch-roofed houses tended by donkeys. Tied at the water's edge are 12-metre long pirogues, canoe-shaped hulls brilliantly painted in primary colours with complex designs. Children paddle in the river and women wash clothes. It's like suddenly appearing in someone's backyard. They cheer and dance on the shore, pleading for photos of their latest diving stunts, and launch themselves off pirogue stems and jetties with intrepid attempts at flight. The whole effect is one of warm domesticity, a far cry from the menacing tribes of old that ravaged, stole from and slaughtered early explorers.

We weave between fish nets that seem to be stretched the full width of the river. More than 150 kilometres deep into the Gambia the terrain begins to change. The river narrows and banks become ominously dark with thick vegetation that hangs dense and dank over the crawling brown

223

water. Strange calls emanate from the jungle and the egrets that have been strutting the shallows now fly fast in close formation as if running a deadly gauntlet. My stomach turns in excitement and a little trepidation – although it's possible it's just the lingering effects of the funny-tasting chicken I bought in a Banjul market yesterday.

The river stretches out like a long hallway leading to an unimaginable room. With every inch our anticipation grows. Every murmur is a speculation as to what awaits at the other end. I imagine it held even greater lure in its early colonial history. It was thought that the Gambia River joined the Niger and could provide a shortcut to Timbuktu and its magnificent trading wealth. Discovering this link became an obsession for the British, who sent party after party of explorers to their deaths searching for it.

The first expedition left in 1618, hoping to find gold. They ventured just under 500 kilometres up-river before being massacred by hostile tribes. The second attempt was utterly fruitless. In 1790 Irishman Major Houghton sailed up the river; his last despatch read, 'Major Houghton's

Villages along the Gambia depend upon the river for food, transport and trade.

compliments – Is in good health on his way to Timbuctoo, [but] robbed of all his goods.' He was never heard of again.

Mungo Park arrived in 1805, determined to find the mouth of the Niger or die in the attempt. He succeeded only in the latter achievement. He reported, 'I am sorry to say...that of the forty-four Europeans who left the Gambia in perfect health, five only are at present alive,' and weeks later he and his remaining entourage were slaughtered close to their goal in present-day Nigeria.

The horror of tropical disease and mutilation haunted successive expeditions and in fact, of any group of Europeans newly arrived on this coast of Africa in the eighteenth century, up to 75 per cent died within their first year. West Africa quickly became known as White Man's Grave. Joseph Conrad embellished the theme in his novel *Heart of Darkness*, depicting the harrowing journey of Marlow up a river: 'I looked around, and I don't know why, but I assure you that never, never before, did this land, this river, this jungle, the very arch of this blazing sky, appear to me so hopeless and so dark, so impenetrable to human thought, so pitiless to human weakness.'

Brady, an enthusiastic Canadian with the facility for a spellbinding tale, has spent all morning convincing us of the swarms of killer bugs that would surely infest every orifice upon landfall. And while we laughed off his warnings, I now find myself slapping the back of my neck and searching the air for imaginary insects. Could it be that the rainforest is already beginning to reel in my mind? How long will it be before jungle claustrophobia, bugs and heat combine to whip the *Starship* crew into a mutinous fervour? Will we all go mad?

A small expedition party leaps into the tender to travel ahead of the ship, radioing back coordinates of obstructions. Michael guns the screaming engines and the boat leaps from the muddy water, an advance party raging up-river. I hang the video camera over the bow of the speeding tender with the base skimming the surface and get a camera angle that captures the exhilaration one feels in the boat, on the river, in the heart of West Africa's White Man's Grave. I'm rather proud of a device I have invented to allow me to do this. I think I'll call it the Frankham.

It's a plastic bag with a hole in one end, but it did take some time to cut the millimetre-accurate circle through a sticker (so the plastic won't tear) to fit perfectly over the lens of the camera. At the other end of the bag is a zip-lock opening for changing tapes, but all the controls can be manipulated through the plastic bag.

Two hundred kilometres from the start of our journey we approach a series of islands. A sign swinging loosely from rusty bolts announces our arrival in the River Gambia National Park. The thick brown tide diverts reluctantly around the islands, which huddle like three sleeping giants. The late-afternoon light gilds a thick cloak of wild date palms. Somewhere in there are chimpanzees...and they're probably watching us. It makes me wonder why they call it Baboon Island.

We take the southern channel and run along the shore of the mainland to a small dock. Stella, wearing a yellow-and-white striped shirt and a straw hat, shades her fair Welsh complexion from the fierce sun as she steps onto the wharf. It has been some time since her last visit to Africa. She has lived in the Gambia for most of her life, and founded the Chimpanzee Rehabilitation Project in 1974 as a solution for a group of confiscated orphan chimps. But since 1981 she has been living in the United Kingdom with her family, returning frequently to direct the project. She smiles broadly as she stands next to her thatched sleeping house, floating on a platform of plastic jerry cans.

The camp is simple. Accommodations, a couple of large cages for housing chimpanzees and a kitchen, all under corrugated-iron roofs. Macaque monkeys scatter noisily around the yard.

The river is as calm as a skating rink and the sun is going down on well-greased tracks. Greens fade to black and the mass of vegetation lining the river becomes horribly alien. The wild sounds of the night begin. It's still warm.

THE AFRICAN SPOROBOLUS grass is luminous yellow, as if Rumpelstiltskin spun it himself. Just a little up-river from the camp, Stella calls three very special guests to breakfast. Beng, Frankie and Diao have been brought here for reintroduction into the wild on the islands of River Gambia

National Park, but it seems they are more interested in film-making.

Diao balances skilfully on the fluidly moving head of the video tripod, clutching on with three hands, and reaches out to seize the spare camera Michael has slung over his shoulder. The tripod tilts forward, pitching the ape onto the ground. Diao looks distinctly bemused, as if the experience has upset everything he knows about trees.

Frankie stares directly into the camera with both hands on the hood; her eyes are keen, captivating and have the same allure that makes you want to know what another person is thinking. She kisses the lens. That will make a nice edit, I think to myself.

Even the youngest chimps have fine white beards as if wise beyond their years. Their ears are over-sized and their faces wrinkled like their skin suit is a couple of sizes too large. We do our best to keep them calm, using soft voices and moving slowly because these kids can get seriously out of control when excited.

Diao piles himself head first into Stella's lap. She picks through his wiry black hair, smacking her lips as if eating. He closes his eyes tightly in obvious pleasure, and the resemblance to my species becomes inescapable – but not unbelievable, because around 98.4 per cent of Diao's

genes are identical to mine. That's a closer genetic relationship than African elephants share with Indian elephants.

Stella believes the likeness is not just genetic. 'The similarities between chimpanzees and humans are numerous. You see the rudimentary buds of all human emotions: jealousy, ambition, compassion.' Frankie pats my leg for attention while I'm trying to film Beng, and Stella goes on, 'And there are incredible politics in chimpanzee society.'

The social politics of the national park community will have to be carefully sculpted if there is to be any chance of restoring these three chimps to the wild. Stella has already attempted to introduce them into the other troop in the park but failed. She believes a longer period of controlled integration is required, and plans to create an enclosure with an electric fence. Members of the community will be assimilated one by one, allowing Frankie, Diao and Beng to make a place for themselves.

BACK IN THE TENDER we forge up the Gambia again. Bugs in my ears, sunburn on my nose. The river twists and turns between densely wooded banks like the spine of a long lean snake. The wind makes my eyes run and Stella's sunhat flap out of control. 'This is the real Africa,' she smiles. 'You half expect to see Humphrey Bogart and the *African Queen* coming the other way.'

Hippopotamuses loll around in the shade of the tangled creepers that choke the riverbank, looking like exotic experiments in buoyancy and volume. They're a monochrome grey, with eyes rimmed pink (like a child who stayed too long in the hotel swimming pool), at least the size and weight of a small car – though considerably more difficult to park. It seems God put the same size ears on chimps and hippos alike as some sort of pre-emptive cost-cutting exercise in his first continent.

The hippos scare the wits out of us on a number of occasions, surfacing close to the tender with a roar of breath. And though the vessel weighs over a tonne, a large bull could capsize it in a flash. Hippos are responsible for more human deaths than any other animal in Africa. They've got a notorious mean streak and we do our best to survey them from a distance.

The tender traces a foamy path along the edge of the island. Stella sits on the bow, scanning the matted rainforest for signs of chimpanzees.

'Why do you do it?' I ask. 'What makes you want to devote your life to looking after these apes?'

Stella searches her mind as she searches the forest, as if she's never articulated the reason. 'I guess I don't have any choice. I was foster mother to a group of chimps, they've grown and been added to and now they're like part of my extended family.' She pauses. 'If I don't look after them nobody else will. The 61 chimps living on this island now would be in a cage or never have existed at all.'

It costs Stella nearly US$40,000 per year to pay four staff and supply medicine to the project. Through the Chimpanzee Rehabilitation Project she is now campaigning for international support to aid her work. Four hundred people from around the world are supporting the project by 'adopting' the chimps in the national park, yet funding is still falling short of running expenses.

In an attempt to make the project self-sustaining, Stella is creating an eco-tourism venture to work in parallel with the rehabilitation work. Visitors will be able to stay in elegant floating lodges on the Gambia and get an insight into the project, the rainforest and the surrounding communities. Stella also hopes that the participation from the local community, along with her own initiatives to start a village clinic and fund education, will encourage villagers to respect the chimpanzee national park. It's a formula that has worked effectively in other developing nations with land-use pressures, and may well see chimps thrive in the Gambia, where the IUCN Red List has registered them extinct for many years.

Date palms rustle, trees tremble, and over the putter of the engines I can hear the vocalisations of great apes. The forest quivers, and the hairs on the back of my neck stand to attention. Fast-moving shadows here and there, commotion in the jungle. We are careful not to get too close to the shore as chimps can leap a surprising distance and once aboard the boat the situation could become dangerous, especially for the ape – chimpanzees cannot swim because their bone density is so high.

Deep dark forest. Shadows and eyes. Shuddering branches. A face appears behind leaves and disappears. Another. 'It's Hexel,' says Stella. 'Hello, sweetheart. Hello, Hexel, we're just stopping to admire you and your family,' she sings.

Hexel, a large dark-skinned female, swaggers out of the bush, extending her arm, palm up, as a greeting. What can only be described as a broad grin develops on her face and she holds the pose, arm reaching towards Stella. The recognition is undeniable and the warmth palpable. Wrapped in Hexel's other arm is her son Henry.

More faces. A whole family leans out of the shadows, examining the strange boat and its human contents, as if drawing profound conclusions about our species. One of the staff begins lobbing baobab fruit to the riverbank and the chimpanzees find courage. From the trees they clamber to the water's edge, seeming equally content swinging from hands or feet. They don't need additional feeding on this island, but once a month rangers will attract chimps to the riverbank with the football-sized fruit to monitor the community.

Another family appears at the shore to feed. The older chimpanzees have very dark complexions, the dominant male a distinctly larger more brutish character with gigantic hands like he's wearing ski gloves. He's over a metre tall and must weigh in excess of 50 kilograms. The hierarchies within the group are clear almost immediately from their interactions, and as Stella fills us in on their histories and relationships, behaviour becomes more predictable.

One cannot underestimate the privilege of witnessing chimpanzees in their natural habitat. Beyond this national park they stand little chance. Wild chimps are now extinct elsewhere in the Gambia and, of the 25 countries that once supported populations, they are now extinct or impossibly depleted in 13. According to the WWF there are only 187,000 still in the wild. The biggest threat is destruction of habitat. Vast tracts of native bush are felled on a daily basis for hardwood and to supply land for monoculture cash crops. Many forests have been fragmented by development into areas too small to ensure the long-term survival of their plant and animal species.

The populations of chimpanzees that do still exist are also under

Nellie, saved by her brother after the death of their mother, has now learned to provide for herself.

tremendous hunting pressure for the illegal bush-meat trade. Once the dietary protein for rural central and west Africans, the meat from endemic rainforest species is in demand in major African cities and by African populations in the cities of Europe. Commercial hunting of chimpanzees outstrips the natural population growth. It's an ugly equation.

Nellie lounges between branches, her wing-nut ears catching the afternoon light. She proudly displays a magnificent paunch. 'She has her mother's eyes,' says Stella, recalling the early days of the project, which began with the introduction of Nellie's mother, Nini, whom Stella used to comfort with lullabies. 'I remember sitting here, more or less in this spot, watching Nini consoling her daughter, rocking her backwards and forwards, patting her back. I thought, my God, that's the lullaby I had sung to her,' tells Stella, reliving the moment. 'It was an incredible moment when I realised something from my own family's culture had been adapted by Nini for her daughter.'

Nini died some years later, leaving her youngest daughter, two-and-a-half-year-old Nellie, alone. Stella was heartbroken – and concerned for Nellie, who was not yet old enough to care for herself. She considered interfering to remove the young chimp until she was able to fend for herself, but then the entire philosophy of reintroduction would be compromised. It was a chimpanzee that provided the solution. Nellie's nine-year-old brother Nelson took responsibility for her, sheltering his young sister during storms and sharing his food. He made the difference between life and death for Nellie and proved the resilience of the chimpanzee community in River Gambia National Park.

'The most rewarding thing is to see these individuals, that have come as distressed infants, now grown up and totally adapted to life on the island with families of their own.' Stella beams positivity in the evening light, though the massive challenge of incorporating Diao, Frankie and Beng into the community still remains.

Even as the muted tones of dusk begin to loom, I know that the sun is only beginning to rise again on the chimpanzees of River Gambia National Park. Out of a disparate and desperate collection of troubled youth, Stella has created a community capable of sustaining itself.

SINCE OUR VISIT there has been a lot of activity in the Chimpanzee Rehabilitation Project. Using the electric-fenced enclosure, an attempt was made to introduce the three young chimps to the main community in the national park. Diao was successfully introduced and seems to be integrating well, but Frankie refused to have anything to do with the park population and had to be extracted. It was feared she might get hurt or killed by the others. Sadly, Beng died from enteritis before even beginning the process of introduction. Nellie continues to do well and no longer depends upon the care of her brother Nelson.

And there are changes for Stella as well. She has been balancing motherhood commitments across two continents and two species for 20 years. But now she's found a solution. 'It's a bit hectic here,' she says on the phone from the UK, with the sound of packing boxes crashing in the background. 'We sold the house on Monday.' Now that their own children are grown, Stella and her husband David are moving their lives 4000 kilometres south to devote themselves permanently to their other family of primates, in Africa. 'It's pointless being here when we should be in the Gambia, there's just so much to do.'

THE *STARSHIP* CREW is on the move as well. From the Gambia we head north to Senegal, where the women of Yarakh Beach have banded together to sell their fish over the internet, just to compete with the European conglomerates that were destroying their market. But first they had to learn how to read.

And north again with a strong current pushing us towards Europe and the trade winds endeavouring to hold us back. Wind against current; the waves stack up and we get pounded in the worst conditions we have endured yet. We ship blue water over the bow. The wind increases to force 7 and just before noon on the third day of the passage we hear an almighty crack. The 1000-kilogram tender has broken clean through its tie-downs and smashed the cradle to splinters. The ship is slowed to a crawl and in harnesses we secure the wreckage, about-turn and run for cover. The nearest haven – almost the only safe one – is Nouadhibou, a crook in the coast of sunny Mauritania, a nation devoured by the Sahara. A string of 200 abandoned ships quietly rusts in the sea off the shore of Cap Blanc.

Over the next 12 hours the cradle is repaired, the tender refastened and a centimetre of Sahara sand accretes on the side decks. But a few seconds after weighing anchor *Starship* comes to a shuddering halt on a shipwreck just beneath the surface. I leap over the side with a dive bottle, the cold Atlantic stinging my face, to inspect the damage. It's not bad, no cracks or cause for concern, but I take the precaution of sending a digital photograph back to Europe for a quick appraisal. We get the green light within an hour and head out to sea.

The wind has abated but the swell remains angry and for ten days we pitch and pound our way north. Seasickness gets to all of us. By the end of the passage our

Active page 233
Out-take: read about the fisherwomen of Senegal.

Starship pounds up the coast of Mauritania. (Photo: James Frankham)

Captain Martin has lost 6 kilograms. At 2.30 am, just hours before landfall in the Balearic Islands, the bell rings – 'Fire!' We are mustered from our sleep. But what looks like smoke through the engine room camera is in fact steam. The fan failed, the engine overheated and blew a gasket. Now we roll in the Mediterranean for four hours while the engineer restores power. The boat is as tired as we are.

THE ELBE RIVER slithers green under the hull. The past months have seen an urgent consolidation of the 50,000 images and 600 hours of video shot over three years. And now, just minutes before arrival at Hamburg, the final port of call of *Starship*, we are asked by hungry media to sum up the experiences of years in a sound bite. Flash bulbs fire, videotape rolls, but this time the lenses are pointing at us. Thousands of well-wishers line the dock, waving banners and cheering. We had not expected this. Arrival is imminent, the future uncertain, and the past holds a glorious mountain of experience, too enormous to communicate in one moment. The voyage has been part of my life for so long and in a few minutes it will be over. And despite the celebrations, it feels a bit like losing an old friend.

WILD GUIDE

Access to the project site, and to the River Gambia National Park, is strictly limited to those who have either a scientific interest or a clearly defined fund-raising role for the project. In all cases visitors must apply through the Chimpanzee Rehabilitation Trust for a permit from the Director of Department of Parks and Wildlife Management. However Stella is developing a very small eco-tourism project that will be able to accommodate eight people in small floating lodges, directly on the upper reaches of the River Gambia, but outside the official park boundaries. It is

hoped that income from this venture will be able to sustain the rehabilitation project. Stella is also funding a village clinic and a school sponsorship scheme so that locals derive some direct benefit from the conservation activities. Keep tabs on the progress of this project using www.wildlands.cc at the beginning of this book. In the meantime the project is funded by a chimp 'adoption' scheme. For information on that take a look at the Chimpanzee Rehabilitation Trust website or contact Joanne Fielder of the Chimpanzee Rehabilitation Trust (see overleaf).

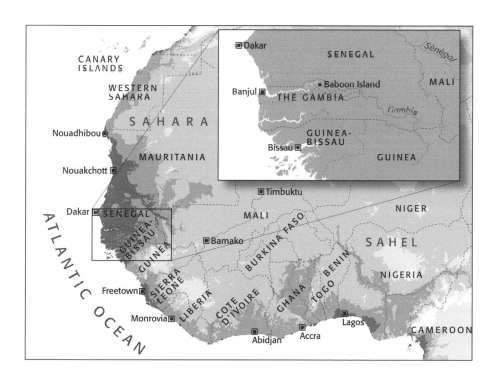

CONTACT

Joanne Fielder
Chimpanzee Rehabilitation Trust
6 Highmoor Cross
Henley-on-Thames
R69 5DP
United Kingdom
Tel: +44-1242-675 720
Email: crt@jdmar.freeserve.co.uk

FURTHER READING

Stella Brewer, *The Forest Dwellers*,
  Collins, 1978

WEBSITES

Chimpanzee Rehabilitation Trust
  www.chimprehab.com
Hidden Gambia
  www.hiddengambia.com

Following pages *p. 237* Diao, always confident with other chimps, has been successfully reintroduced to the park community. *p. 238 (top)* Stella (here with Frankie and Beng) believes that for normal social development orphaned chimpanzees need a strong relationship with a mother, even if the mother must be human. *p. 238 (bottom)* Hexel and Henry relax in the park. *p. 239* Cap Blanc, Nouadhibou, is a graveyard for abandoned ships. (Photo: James Frankham)

fiordland
NEW ZEALAND

TUTERAKIWHANOA lashed at the land with his digging stick and shouted his powerful karakia chant. The sea crashed into each great lesion and formed long reaches of water between the mighty cliffs. With every stroke of his ko, Tuterakiwhanoa became more accurate, each valley a little straighter than the first. In this way he carved 13 mighty fiords in New Zealand's deep south before settling back to admire his craftsmanship.

This is the creation story of Fiordland according to indigenous New Zealanders. Maori call this place Ata-whenua, the land of shadows. Geologists believe that Tuterakiwhanoa's legendary stick was a series of

Left 'White-tip' and her calf ride on *Starship*'s pressure wave up Doubtful Sound. (Photo: James Frankham)

glacier advances from the island's massive backbone 2 million years ago. It's undeniably one of the most rugged regions in the country and is protected both as a World Heritage site and New Zealand's largest national park, covering more than 1 million hectares of wilderness.

Maori arrived a thousand years ago from the Pacific, making New Zealand the last major landmass to be settled by humans. For 800 years they visited Fiordland on hunting sorties and collected the prized New Zealand jade, pounamu. When the British explorer Captain James Cook saw this fiord in 1770 he wrote, 'The land on each side of the entrance of this harbor riseth almost perpendicularly from the Sea to a very considerable height, and this was the reason why I did not attempt to go in with the Ship because I saw clearly that no winds could blow there but what was either right in or right out.'

The sheer walls of Doubtful Sound climb perilously to summits of well over 1000 metres and plunge into the depths for 400 metres. The cliffs of the fiord are steep, rugged and covered with dense rainforest. And this far south the low sun barely penetrates the yawning elbows of Doubtful, which is instead filled with clouds and rain.

More than 7 metres of rain falls here annually, 200 days a year, turning the hillsides to wild waterfalls and covering the sea water with a layer of fresh water up to 16 metres thick. This layer is stained tea-brown with tannins from the rainforest, allowing light to penetrate only a few metres underwater. Many species of deep-ocean fish, as well as rare black coral usually found at a depth of more than 100 metres, are found in Fiordland in just 20 metres of water.

Two years ago my time on *Starship* started with a cruise through these fiords, and now I am back in New Zealand after exploring 25 countries, in this place where I began. It is a return to familiar landscapes, but with a fresh desire to learn more about my own country. On that first visit bottlenose dolphins rode *Starship*'s bow wave for an hour and a half up Doubtful Sound, all the way to where water meets land in Deep Cove. They were battleship grey and similarly robust, with permanent grins behind snubby snouts. Mothers and calves alike bundled around the bulbous bow. Occasionally one appeared to rest its fluke on the hull to glide motionless with its dorsal fin cutting through the water, perfectly balanced against the pressure wave. They twisted and turned, rolled and breached the surface in obvious pleasure. And if I listened carefully above the rush of water on the bow, above the low thrum of *Starship*'s engine, I could make out squeaks and whistles, perhaps cries of delight in dolphin-speak.

IT'S 8 AM in Doubtful Sound and though the sun has risen somewhere, it hasn't penetrated the heavy cloak of cloud, the sheets of rain and the deep walls of Hall Arm. It's still dark and may be for some time. Oli's brow is furrowed in concentration. He leans over the side of the aluminium boat, staring into the depths, his eyes focused somewhere at the end of the thick black cable in his right hand. His knuckles are white, water drips off the end of his nose and he's drenched from his soggy thermal hat to his gumboots, which slosh around in inches of rainwater that has collected in the bilge.

I slip and slide around on the rocks, trying to get a photograph that will measure the hardship Oliver Boisseau has faced to record his data. The camera is covered with a plastic bag, through which pokes the lens. I have torn a small aperture around the viewfinder but it goes foggy when I put my eye to it. There's no light to focus by, and it's so cold the camera batteries have declared some kind of electric mutiny and gone to sleep for the winter.

It's at this point – cold, wet and photograph-less – that we discover the tide has fallen and the boat has come to rest on a large round rock. And no amount of shoving from the shore will set it free. It soon seems inevitable that Oli and I will have to get a lot deeper in Fiordland than we had hoped. I take my boots off.

Meltwater flows off the snowy peaks 2000 metres above us, tumbles down the sides of the fiord and sits in a layer of freezing fresh. I don't know what temperature the water is, but it stings my bare feet and they turn a dramatic shade of red before going numb. It's a bit of a relief when they completely lose sensation, though it makes me clumsy. We scramble around up to our thighs, avoiding the depths that would expose

Bottlenose dolphins can grow to 4 metres in length but the most southerly individuals are known to have smaller fins and more robust bodies. (Photo: James Frankham)

our nether regions to the painful effects of icy water. Finally after many a momentous push we despatch the vessel back into the fiord.

Oli takes it in his stride. For the past three years he has been working tirelessly, battling against weather, geography and the whims of wild bottlenose dolphins just so that he can hear them talk.

'It's like trying to learn Russian without a phrasebook,' explains Oli, a British smirk developing on his semi-frozen face. 'But now I can associate vocalisations with specific behaviour.'

After thousands of hours of observation, numerous dorsal fin photos and playback through reels of recorded dolphin vocalisations, Oli has begun to decipher dolphin language. He has defined 14 unique types of vocalisation from clicks – largely used for navigation – to tonal whistles and low-frequency calls that can travel up to 20 kilometres through water. Often these whistles, creaks and buzzes are combined into long styros, or sequences, much like human sentences. It seems that dolphins from different pods use different dialects and Oli is now so attuned to the nuances of dolphin-speak that he can actually differentiate between recordings of different pods, based simply on the structure of their calls.

The majority of the dolphin brain is dedicated to processing acoustic information. It's a super-computer for sound many times more advanced than state-of-the-art human-built sonar systems. It is so sophisticated that researchers believe dolphins can use the vocalisations of other dolphins, as well as their own echoes, to build up a complex three-dimensional image of their environment. This 'passive-sonar' is used intensively when feeding.

The fiords offer a unique opportunity to study the lives of dolphins. Within the confines of Doubtful Sound, Oli can study the social structure of a single group year-round, and this pod has been researched intensively for nearly a decade.

'This pod is really unique and I have got to know them all intimately.' Oli pauses thoughtfully. 'Other groups I have studied have been transitory, but this one is very different for me…it's been a huge learning curve.'

Two years ago there was a split in the 60-strong pod. A young male called Gallatin took a group of 20-odd males and broke away from the rest of the pod led by Jonah. For some time the groups remained apart, living and feeding in different arms of the fiord. One day it all came to a head – perhaps young Gallatin was making a bid for control of the whole pod. For 47 minutes the two groups of dolphins duelled, biting, slapping and pounding with their tails. The leaders, Jonah and Gallatin, were particularly involved, leaping from the water and clashing heads in mid-air. A few months down the track they put aside their differences and the pod regrouped, though Oli believes Gallatin is merely biding his time before attempting another coup.

This is the second most-southerly group of bottlenose dolphins in the world, beaten by just a few nautical miles by a pod in Dusky Sound. Fiordland dolphins are larger and more robust than their tropical cousins, and have smaller fins and tails to reduce surface area to volume ratio. They are at the edge of their range and have learnt to breed seasonally, rather than year-round as in warmer climes. Typically there will be two or three new calves each year, born when the fresh water layer in the fiord has been heated in the summer sun.

'The dolphins in Doubtful Sound have the privilege of escaping fishing nets and pollution, but they're really up against the elements,' explains Oli. 'They're living on a knife-edge – most of their movements are motivated purely by water temperature.' In the 2001/2002 seasons five calves were born to the pod, but none survived the year. Perhaps fishing pressure outside the fiord limited food supply for the dolphins, perhaps the water was too cold. Whatever the case, the numbers in the pod are decreasing. In the last five years the population has gone from 65 down to 50.

It's a special day for the soggy Brit and his hydrophone. After three full years in Fiordland, Oli is plying the sound for the last time.

'I guess I will miss the dolphins. You become very personally involved in the research.' He pulls alongside the fishing boat *Aorere* and, as I hurdle over the gunwale toting packs of defunct camera equipment, adds, 'It's the perfect lifestyle, but you can't live all your life in the field.' A smile breaks through his cold, wet countenance. 'But to work in an office would be a living death for me.'

SHORTY SLINGS MY GEAR aboard *Aorere*. Rain runs down his face and pills in his grey whiskers. 'It's a bit damp,' he quips as we seek shelter in the foggy windowed wheelhouse. In truth the downpour hasn't ceased in six days.

Aorere is a solid 14-metre fishing boat with a small wheelhouse amidships. Two masts, tangled with rigging and lifting gear, are used more for working lines and swinging dinghies than setting sails. A diesel stove rumbles warm in the corner, the longwave radio squelches quietly and a throbbing engine pounds away below decks, pushing us toward the fiord entrance. We make a modest 7 knots, the good ship leaving barely a trace in the water.

Shorty has been fishing the coast of New Zealand since 1967, many years before I was born. He puts salt on his food, sugar in his coffee and whispers 'Lovely' after the first mouthful of a cold beer, epitomising the southern gentleman: rugged and charming. We speculate about the weather because forecasts are hard to come by – even the long arms of SSB radio don't reach into the cavernous fiords – and fishermen rely on news from boats further out to sea where the reception is better. I have little to add to the meteorological intelligence, but I feel the lob of a swell under the keel, a portent of a massive sea at the entrance, still an hour away.

'Fishermen around here have a lot of respect for this place,' says Shorty, rolling his orange tartan Swanndri shirt up at the sleeves, 'Most have been fishing in these parts for years, and know how to look after it.'

In fact a group of fishermen was instrumental in drafting a management plan for the fiords, and though some environmentalists don't believe it goes far enough, all are impressed by what is a very positive step forward. There is now no commercial fishing in Doubtful and Milford Sounds,

Sealers arrived in 1792 in Dusky Sound, and by 1830 had eliminated fur seals from most of their range. The population is now returning. (Photo: James Frankham)

and strict limits on non-commercial activity. And as well as no-take zones that stretch over many nautical miles, small 'china shops' conserve discrete areas of diverse or abundant life.

But causing the most damage to coral trees below the waterline are the trees above it. A large beech tree coming unstuck at the top of a high fiord wall can sweep away hundreds of others on the way down and avalanche into the sea, continuing the path of destruction all the way down to the seafloor. And while the bush above will regenerate over a couple of decades, the coral beneath may take centuries.

Possums and deer destabilise the hillsides and kill the trees, adding to the problem of tree avalanches. The possums were introduced to begin a fur trade in 1858 and now 70 million of the little devils chew through 20,000 tonnes of fruit and vegetation every night. Along with other introduced pests, they have transformed the ecology of the New Zealand wilderness forever.

There was a song I learnt as a child:

There was an old lady who swallowed a bird,
How absurd to swallow a bird,
She swallowed the bird to eat the spider
That wriggled and giggled and squiggled inside her,
She swallowed the spider to eat the fly,
I don't know why she swallowed a fly,
Perhaps she'll die.

The macabre lyrics find resonance in the colonial ecology of Fiordland. Rats were introduced, first by the Maori, then by Europeans, who felt pretty bad about it. So they introduced stoats to eat the rats but the native birdlife proved at least as appetising. The stoats ran amuck, proving more destructive by far than the rats. And the rats are still a problem.

New Zealand was one of the first landmasses to separate from the Gondwanaland super-continent 80 million years ago, and with the absence of ground-dwelling predators many species of bird lost the ability to fly. New Zealand's most distinctive birdlife – kiwi, takahe, weka and kakapo – is flightless. And thanks to the introduction of stoats, rats, cats and dogs, also endangered.

The charismatic kakapo has become the flagship of conservation efforts. The massive flightless parrots were once widely distributed throughout the country but were hunted by the Maori and devoured by introduced rats and dogs. By the time Europeans arrived the bird was largely gone from the North Island. Stoats killed the South Island kakapo and consumed their eggs until in 1957 there were no known kakapo in the world. In the 1970s a desperate rescue mission found a population of 15 birds in Fiordland, lifted them out of the forest by helicopter and whisked them away to offshore enclaves free of introduced predators.

Aboard Shorty's fishing boat we begin a two-day passage from Doubtful Sound to one of New Zealand's most protected outposts of conservation, Chalky Island. It's a wind-whipped fortress on the south-west tip of the country, deep in the bowels of nowhere. There are no roads and the one-hour helicopter flight is highly weather-dependent. Going by boat is no soft option either – this corner of New Zealand is by far the most notorious stretch of coast in the country and there have been gale warnings for the last eight days straight. But today the seas are a mere 3 metres and only 25 knots of wind hammers the coast.

Aorere plugs on up the winding fiord, ocean waves beginning to lash at the hull. We pass through the bottleneck between Secretary Island and the mainland and the swell stacks up against the outgoing tide. *Aorere* lurches and rolls, casting sprawling arcs of salt water. Spume rolls down the side decks. I can feel the narcosis of seasickness rolling in the pit of my stomach.

I manage to keep down my lunch for three hours rolling around in the briny before *Aorere* ducks for cover behind Resolution Island. Shorty pilots her down a back road, through the narrow Acheron Passage, a long calm bowling alley that leads to Dusky Sound. Rain patters on the deck again, turning the sky grey and the distance hazy. Dusky looks a little morose, sullen, sulking away her isolation.

'She's well named "Dusky",' muses Shorty. 'She spends a fair bit of time looking like this.'

Shorty pilots *Aorere* out of Dusky Sound. All is calm – for now. (Photo: James Frankham)

Dolphins escort us to the deep dark water of the fiord. It's 4 pm and the light is fading, the mountains are swamped in pleats of low cloud. We tie up alongside a floating provision shed in Cascade Cove, one of a handful of locations where fishermen cache supplies. Most of these floating stockpiles are laden with ropes, cray-pots and spare buoys, but many have additional features like a bar and satellite TV so the cray boys can watch the rugby.

For the humble crew of *Aorere* it's roast beef and vegies, beer ('Lovely') and a weather report. The HF radio hisses and crackles on 4146 Megahertz, 'Gale warning in force. South-west 35 tonight tending north-west in morning.' Shorty raises his eyes optimistically as if 35 knots is a zephyr. 'Sea very rough. South-west swell 3 metres, rising. North-west swell two metres, easing. Poor visibility and rain.'

A strong wind slaps waves against the hull as I try to go to sleep. But there's a glassy calm in the morning, save for the raindrops pattering the surface. It's a surprise spell in the weather and we make a run for Chalky Inlet before the predicted north-west wind gains breath.

The nor'wester catches up as we round Cape Providence, great squalls ripping through at 35 knots, streaking the confused sea with veins of white foam. Spray pummels the cabin windows. The sea mounts up in liquid hills that come crashing down on the foredeck. Some time ago we slipped off the range of the electronic chart, leaving only the GPS waypoints of Shorty's favourite fishing spots. I feel far from home.

With the combined effects of rain and spray we can see barely 10 metres. The radar loses range inexplicably and we're left blind. I take rough coordinates off a paper chart and call out the longitude and latitude to Shorty, who does his best to steer the course, his nose pressed against the glass searching for breaking water. We must be within 50 metres of the reef that skirts the north-west coast of Chalky Island, but we can't see it. To make an error now would be deadly. 'You wouldn't read about it,' calls Shorty over the howl of wind in the rigging, then glances at me fervently scrawling in my field notebook. 'I'm hoping you will!' I call back.

The rain abates and the wind eases a little as we tuck into the lee of Chalky Island. Steep white cliffs rim most of the mighty citadel and scrub, contoured by the fierce wind, clings to the tops. On the north-eastern corner is a lonely hut buried deep in the trees.

Jason Hamill is the only human inhabitant of Chalky Island. 'You'll have to land on the rocks,' he calls out, bobbing around in a whitewater kayak. 'The beach is too rough.'

The transfer is finally achieved by rowing a plastic dinghy through the whitewater and leaping with the camera gear over a rising wave onto the rocks.

'Welcome to Chalky Island,' beams Jason. I breathe a sigh of relief.

He asks me to unpack my bags inside the hut, to check for rodents and unseen nasties. The eradication programme to free the island of stoats has been expensive and time consuming, so Jason maintains uncompromising quarantine standards. Chalky was deliberately set up as the sexiest place on earth for one very valuable male, Richard Henry.

He is the last of the Fiordland kakapo and represents an important source of genetic variation. He must be given the greatest chance to pass on his rare DNA, so staff have placed Richard Henry here with the most fertile females and subordinate males who won't cramp his style.

Dusk descends like a cold blanket on Chalky. We don thermals and Gore-Tex, head torches, packs and boots. Jason and I are about to go looking for one of 19 perfectly camouflaged parrots in 514 hectares of dense rainforest. And it's dark. We start off on the aptly named rollercoaster track. It climbs and descends through several hundred vertical metres of muddy inclines, making for tough going, and I puff under the weight of camera gear.

We're looking for Trevor, a four-year-old male transferred to Chalky Island just recently. Jason wants to weigh him to make sure he is settling in to his new home well. Stopping for a moment at the top of one particularly lofty hill, Jason assembles a device that looks like a TV antenna. Holding it over his head, he tunes a VHF radio receiver on his belt. It beeps. And Jason smiles. 'He's a bit closer to the beach,' he announces with conviction.

The Kakapo Recovery Programme is an intensive, high-tech response to a conservation emergency. The Department of Conservation staff use VHF telemetry to find and monitor kakapo in the wild. They are tracked every four days and weighed with electronic scales hidden at feeding stations. And when breeding season kicks off, an unparalleled level of surveillance takes place. A video camera is mounted in each nest, complete with an infrared doorbell. When the female leaves the nest at night to feed, a human volunteer sleeping in a tent 50 metres away is alerted. The volunteer goes to the nest and keeps the eggs warm with a miniature electric blanket until the female returns. Every movement is radioed back to a central nest controller.

Active page 252
Hear the boom of a kakapo. Download the audio clip.

Using aggressive conservation techniques like this, the programme has succeeded in raising 24 new chicks in a single season. This grand success increases the number of kakapo in the country by

150 per cent, enough to change the IUCN Red List classification from critically endangered to simply endangered, with a four-year probationary period.

Jason and I have been sitting around in the mud and rain for a couple of hours now and the novelty is beginning to wear off. Closer to the beach, the bush is thinner and has an unsettling Blair Witch ambience. Eerie barks of fur seals echo through the forest and every now and again one comes crashing through the dark bush, scaring the wits out of me.

My thermals itch, my gear is wet and one of my boots has ripped open at the back. Mud squelches around my instep; breath condenses and lingers in the glow of the headlamp. Jason raps on a plastic feeding container and calls out 'Hello Trevor' in a sing-song tone. 'He's pretty close,' assures Jason. 'We'll just wait here.'

I'm sitting on a muddy track at midnight on a near-deserted island at 47 degrees south waiting for a rare parrot to come bounding out of the bush to play.

'Hello Trevor.'

My guide has lost touch with reality. It seems he has spent too much time on his own. Surely this find-a-parrot-with-an-antenna deal is an elaborate hoax.

Active page 254
Out-take: see more
photos of the
remarkable kakapo.

'Hello Trevor.'

There's a crackle in the bush and a feathery face appears between the ferns. Hello Trevor. A plump bird slowly emerges from the undergrowth, picking his way towards the track. He's about the size of a Swiss ball, standing half a metre high with thick strong feet the size of my own hands.

Trevor takes a step at a time, measuring his nerve, strutting along the muddy trail with his head bobbing in time. He walks past me with barely a glance to Jason, whose arm is outstretched with his secret weapon, a piece of apple. Trevor leans forward. Doctor Dolittle assures him softly, 'Hello Trevor.'

Trevor looks like a big budgie, beautiful variegated feathers with a dozen striking shades of greens and a musky aroma. I guess I was expecting a more fragile-looking critter, a poor primitive bird at an evolutionary dead end. Instead I see Trevor, bold as brass, both beautiful and robust, healthy, game and inquisitive. He wrestles with Jason's apple and romps around in the manuka trees with the energy and charisma of a great survivor, marvellously adapted to a particular way of life.

The rescue of the fat flightless parrot of Fiordland represents the fundamental tenets of conservation. The existence of kakapo is of little direct benefit to humans; they are unlikely to be seen by tourists for at least 50 years, they contribute nothing to the New Zealand economy and very little to the environment. But we keep them alive, aware that it was humans that were responsible for their decline. We preserve because we ought to. We protect the environment because we know we should.

Trevor suddenly stands bolt upright, glances at Jason and trots off into the bush like he's late for a meeting. 'He's funny like that,' smirks Jason. 'Every kakapo has a unique personality but this one seems to have half a dozen.'

Suddenly the bush is quiet again, overcrowded with shadows and rain.

WILD GUIDE

Fiordland National Park's 1.2 million hectares are criss-crossed by 500 kilometres of well-maintained walking tracks linking 60 huts. The huts are maintained by the Department of Conservation, from which you can purchase hut passes at an admirably affordable rate. It is some of the best trekking in the world. The large chunks of Fiordland not reached by the tracks are inaccessible to all but the most adventurous – or those with a helicopter.

GETTING THERE

A road runs to Milford Sound, a dramatic, yet intensively touristed fiord in the north of the national park. Getting to Doubtful Sound is harder: it involves taking a boat across Lake Manapouri and then a specialised bus for the journey to Deep Cove. Real Journeys runs all of these services and also runs tourist boats into the fiords. Try to get a break in the weather but be warned that, in the words of Alex the coach

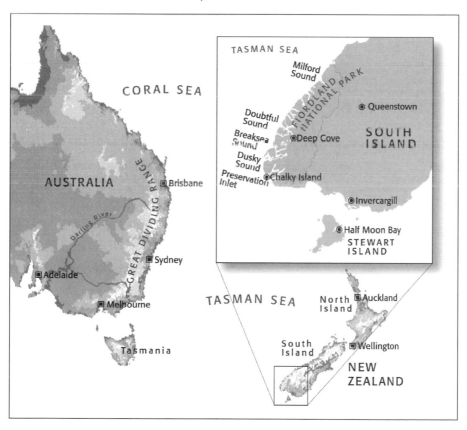

driver, 'It only rains twice a week here; the first time for three days and the second for four.' Lance and Ruth Shaw take passengers on multi-night cruises in the fiords and diving excursions to the harder-to-reach places.

CONTACTS
Real Journeys
PO Box 1
Lakefront
Te Anau
New Zealand
Freephone: 0800 65 65 01 (within NZ)
Tel: +64-3-249 7416
Fax: +64-3-249 7022
Email: reservations@realjourneys.co.nz

Lance Shaw
Fiordland Ecology Holidays
PO Box 40
Manapouri
Tel: +64-03-249 6600
Email: info@fiordland.gen.nz

FURTHER READING
Derek Grzelewski, 'Bird on the Brink', *New Zealand Geographic*, Issue 56, 2002

David Butler, *Quest for the Kakapo*, Heinemann Reed, 1989

Ralph Powlesland, *Kakapo Search on Stewart Island*, Department of Conservation, 1988

Neville Peat and Brian Patrick, *Wild Fiordland: Discovering the Natural History of a World Heritage Area*, University of Otago Press, 1996

Kennedy Warne and Frans Lanting, 'HotSpots: New Zealand', *National Geographic*, October 2002

Douglas Adams, *Last Chance to See*, Ballantine Books, 1992

WEBSITES
Kakapo Recovery Programme
 www.kakaporecovery.org.nz
Department of Conservation
 www.doc.govt.nz
New Zealand Trust for Conservation
Volunteers
 www.conservationvolunteers.org.nz
Real Journeys
 www.fiordlandtravel.co.nz
Fiordland EcoCharters
 www.fiordland.gen.nz
Destination Fiordland Travel Information
 www.fiordland.org.nz

Following pages *p. 257* Boomer, a female kakapo found in thick scrub at 2 am on Chalky Island, was hand-reared as a hatchling and is comfortable around humans. (Photo: James Frankham) *pp. 258–9 Starship* approaches Stirling Falls, which drops 151 metres into Milford Sound. *p. 260* Frigatebirds follow *Starship* as it leaves Darwin Island, Galapagos.

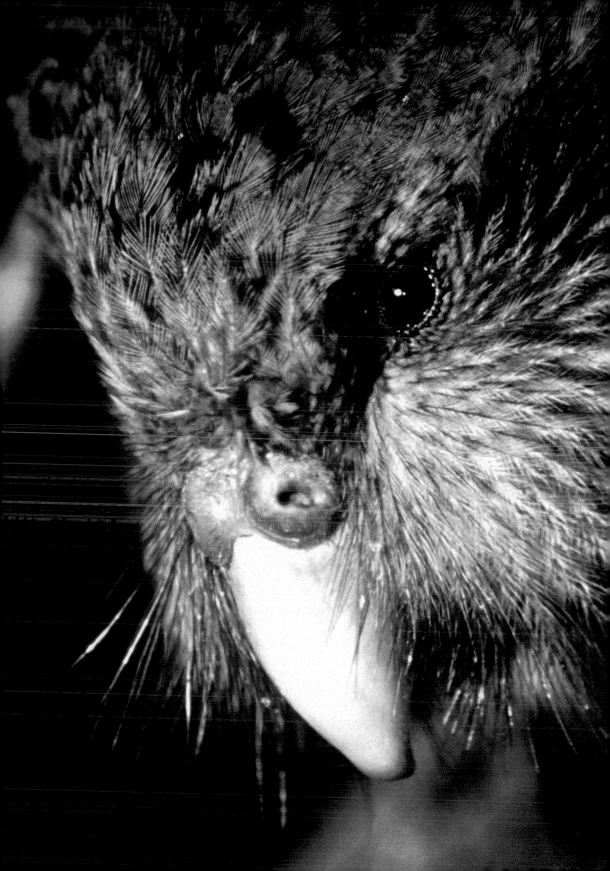